SINGLE FATHER
BETTER DAD

HOW I SURVIVED DIVORCE AND THRIVED

MARK TUCKER

Mark Tucker was born in England and moved to Australia in 2001 with his then wife and two young daughters. He is currently a Partner at a major consulting company and enjoying the challenge of bringing up a blended family of two girls, two boys and three dogs. Mark's passion is to help single fathers become the best dads that they can be.

Single Father, Better Dad: How I Survived Divorce and Thrived
Mark Tucker

Published by Classic Author and Publishing Services Pty Ltd.
Imprint of JoJo Publishing.
First published 2014

'Yarra's Edge'
2203/80 Lorimer Street
Docklands VIC 3008
Australia

Email: jo-media@bigpond.net.au or visit www.classic-jojo.com

Copyright © 2014 Mark Tucker

All rights reserved. No part of this printed or video publication may be reproduced, stored in or introduced into a retrieval system, or transmitted, in any form, or by any means (electrical, mechanical, photocopying, recording or otherwise) without the prior written permission of the publisher and copyright owner.

The information, views, opinions and visuals expressed in this publication are solely those of the author(s) and do not reflect those of the publisher. The publisher disclaims any liabilities or responsibilities whatsoever for any damages, libel or liabilities arising directly or indirectly from the contents of this publication.

JoJo Publishing

Editor: Julie Athanasiou
Designer / typesetter: Working Type Studio (www.workingtype.com.au)
Printed in China by Ink Asia

National Library of Australia Cataloguing-in-Publication entry
Author: Tucker, Mark, 1962- author.
Title: Single father, better dad : how i survived divorce and thrived / Mark Tucker.
ISBN: 9780987588012 (paperback)
Subjects: Tucker, Mark, 1962-
                    Single fathers--Australia--Biography.
                    Single parents--Australia--Biography.
                    Divorced fathers--Australia--Biography.
                    Divorced men--Australia--Biography.
Dewey Number: 306.874220994

DEDICATION

To my 'old' family for helping me through the dark times and to my 'new' family for helping me find my way back to the light. I love you all.

But especially to my daughters for their love and support, and for giving me the inspiration to write this book and, of course, to Alison for writing the next chapter in our lives with me.

"GOODNIGHT, MY LOVE"

"Goodnight, my love."

Three little words.

Three tender words of love.

Three words that any man would love to hear. But these words weren't meant for me. They were meant for someone else. Another man. These weren't tender words of love to warm my heart these were words of betrayal, and they reached out from the sent folder of my wife's mobile phone and formed a circle around my heart. A circle of stone cold dread.

I looked back at her—my wife, the mother of our children—sleeping peacefully in our bed, the first early rays of the new day lighting the room. She looked so normal, so innocent. It was such a familiar and comforting scene. But what was running through her head? Was she dreaming of someone else—of him? And who the bloody hell was this 'him' anyway?

Suddenly, my body's defence mechanisms kicked in, a combination of shock and fear. The cold hand around my heart moved down my body to my stomach, and then to my bowels. For a moment I didn't know whether I was going to be leaning over the toilet or sitting on it, but instead I settled on a series of dry retches and ten laps of the lounge room.

But what next? Should I wake her? What would I say? More importantly, what would she say—and did I want to hear it? This was way too big and way too threatening to think about at 7.15am on a Wednesday morning. It was better to be in denial, so I simply got dressed and went to work. It just seemed the easiest thing to do. I left the house and quietly shut the door behind me. I didn't want to wake my wife or my daughters—as though by letting them sleep the dawn of our new reality wouldn't break.

Was this just a road hump or a fork in the road of our life together?

"Goodnight, my love."

Maybe those three little words were, in some cryptic way, meant for me after all. Were our days together coming to an end? Was this it?

Later that day I suggested to my wife that we meet for a cup of tea. How nice, she said—we haven't done that for ages. I walked to our meeting place, lightheaded, struggling to control the thoughts that were tearing through my mind. People were going about their normal, ordinary business and I wanted them to stop and let me pass in silence and bow their heads. I wanted them to recognise my trauma—this wasn't just another ordinary day for me. For me this was a day filled with foreboding.

And so we met, perhaps for the last time as a 'normal' couple, secret intact. Should I leave things as they were, or should I disturb the wasp's nest? Could I cope with the consequences? I had to ask her.

My wife denied it of course, in fact she was indignant. *Who? Never heard of him! What? Don't be ridiculous!*

But she couldn't deny those three little words. Those three little words of love for one man and betrayal of another. And then confession. It was nothing, she said. It was just something meaningless, she said. She hardly knew him, she said.

But I had to go on, I had to fight my cramping stomach and ask the big questions. Are you sleeping with him? *Of course not!* Are you in love with him? *Don't be stupid!* She made me feel guilty for questioning her loyalty. She made me feel guilty for going through her phone. She was sorry. She didn't want to risk our family over something so trivial.

I shivered, the adrenalin started to ease, stress levels falling as the relief warmed me. I was exhausted and our conversation was exhausted, so I kissed her goodbye and said that I would see her at home. Everything was going to be okay—wasn't it?

We spent a quiet, close, reflective evening together, and later that night we made love. But I felt detached. I felt as though there was someone else in the room. Was he watching us, or was I watching him? I looked at my wife, her eyes closed. Was she imagining I was him? Or wishing I was him? Was he going to be with us every time we made love—casting an ongoing shadow over our bedroom and our marriage?

Everything was going to be okay, I told myself. We would learn from this, I told myself. We would get back on track, I told myself. We would survive—our family would survive.

But I was wrong. Everything wasn't going to be okay. We had made love for the last time. We wouldn't survive. It was the last goodbye.

And that's how it happened for me.

"Goodnight, my love."

1

Dazed and confused

So that's how it happened, and a few days later my wife decided that our marriage was over. I know it's an old cliché, but I genuinely hadn't seen it coming. I had felt that something wasn't quite right—which was why I had trawled the messages on her mobile phone. But I had been looking for a sardine, not a shark. I hadn't expected this in my worst nightmares. I hadn't expected to find something that would be so final.

She had found her 'soul mate' and wanted to be with him, not me. It was a right, royal 'Romeo and Juliet' thing. I hated it. The shock and stress made me feel constantly sick. Seventeen years of marriage over—just like that. "Do not pass Go", "Do not collect $200". I couldn't move that quickly.

I simply didn't understand it. I drove myself mad as I ran mental laps through my head. What had I done wrong? I thought I was a good husband and a good father. I had a good job, I was helpful, I did the washing up, mowed the lawns, ironed my shirts, took the bread out of the freezer—more than a lot of men did I was sure—and, most importantly, I did my bit with the children. I was a 'fun dad'. I refereed the endless games of Monopoly, froze my dangly bits off wading into the sea so that my daughters could swim, sacrificed Saturday mornings to go to netball with my eldest daughter and Saturday afternoons to watch my youngest learning gymnastics. It wasn't always a barrel of laughs but it was what I did. Wasn't all that good enough?

Turns out that it wasn't. Although I was useful around the house, I had not, it was pointed out to me, been a good husband for some time. I had become the marital equivalent of a high-end vacuum cleaner. I was reliable and rarely broke down, I was capable and did what was expected of me, but I wasn't exactly fun to use. Practical, but not exciting or inspiring. My wife didn't want a vacuum cleaner, even if I was Dyson-esq in my dust sucking abilities. She wanted something special, an upmarket espresso machine or pizza maker, with sufficiently heart-aching aesthetic appeal to be an object of desire amongst her friends, combined with the capability to nonchalantly knock out a mouth-watering delicacy at a moment's notice. She wanted the man who could do it all—and apparently her soul mate could, even though he was still in his warranty period and unproven over the long term, and apparently I couldn't.

To be honest, I was a mess. It was all so sudden and so quick. My nice, predictable, stable life had been replaced with one built on total uncertainty and fear. It felt as though the world had become one huge out-of-control fairground ride. My head was spinning and I wanted to get off. I needed something solid to hold on to.

I was desperate to save my marriage. Partly because I was scared (I didn't know what a future on my own might bring), partly because I liked my life (it wasn't always a bed of roses but it was pretty good), but mostly because I didn't want my family to break up. I loved my family and I was proud that we were still together and our children happy, especially when we knew so many other couples who were unhappy or had split up.

I had seen the problems family breakdowns caused, for

children in particular—living in two houses, becoming pawns in nasty disputes between their parents, believing they were to blame for their parents' problems and so on. Also, one of the ex-partners always seemed to come off worse and end up bitter and twisted. I didn't want my kids to go through all that grief and, if I was honest, I didn't want to be the ex-partner that came off worse and ended up bitter and twisted.

Over the next few weeks we talked openly, and maybe honestly, about our feelings. We talked more than we had done for years. Was that part of our problem? I earn my living as a management consultant—so I've been trained to solve problems through the analysis of facts, logic and carefully constructed arguments. But the more we discussed the whys and wherefores of what was happening, the more I recognised that my logical approach was falling on deaf ears. This was an emotional argument. Logic didn't count for anything.

"I've given you everything you've ever wanted," I argued.

A rather bold opening gambit I have to admit. There probably should have been an 'almost' in that first sentence but, undeterred, I continued in a similar vein, listing our achievements.

"We have a good life, we live in a great house, I'm supportive of you, I moved the family from England to Australia for your sake—doesn't all that count for something?"

"It's all true," my wife replied, calmly deflecting my finely thought through argument. "You have been a good husband—but you don't know what I really want or what I really need."

"But we get on so well. We rarely fall out or argue. People say that we make a great couple," I countered.

A nice piece of consulting input from me—bring in an external market reference for validation of the argument.

"We're a good team," she admitted.

An acknowledgement from her, but not in a very positive vein. I kept trying.

"I have always looked after you and put you first."

"You do look after me—but you don't make me feel special," she replied.

We were getting more and more subjective and I was getting more and more desperate. I wanted to get the argument back to the facts again. Surely I couldn't lose with the facts?

"I thought we were happy—I thought you were happy." Now I was getting emotional.

"I am happy—but not happy enough," she offered. Was that subjective or factual? I was starting to get confused.

God it was hard. Who was this stranger? She looked like my wife but what had happened to her? Why was she talking about our marriage being over? Her words were like bricks. Why was she saying these things? She was so certain, so cool, so sure it was the right thing to do. I wanted to grab her and shake her—to make her see the madness of what she was saying. To make her see reality, or at least my reality.

I was desperate. I only had one card left. I knew that it was all or nothing but I also knew that I had to play it.

"I thought you loved me."

"I do love you—but I'm not in love with you."

Fuck—that last one hurt. My all or nothing card had been trumped.

I imagined that this exchange was a bit like facing the fiery fast bowler Brett Lee. It was only a matter of time before one of her deliveries hit me in the nuts—and that last one had hit me hard. Really hard. And it probably had the same effect as being hit in the privates by Brett—a hot, intense streak of pain followed by my eyes welling up, feeling dazed and confused, and completely losing the ability to think clearly or string a sentence together. I could imagine the ball rolling down the inside of my leg and knocking the bails off of my wicket. Was I going to be out? And in such a pathetic fashion?

I had always imagined that, if our marriage were to end, it would be because I had lost my life performing some heroic act to protect my family from a painful and premature death. You know the kind of thing—leaping in front of a runaway truck and pushing them to safety, or saving my children from a house fire only to lose my life when re-entering the burning building to rescue my youngest daughter's hamster. But this? Outdone by some stranger who was better than me in the 'making my wife feel special' department? This wasn't heroic at all.

We continued to talk and talk for day after day. We talked about the impact on us, we talked about the impact on our children and we talked about the impact on our wider families. It was tiring and emotionally exhausting. But worse for me— because I was losing the argument. My attempts at 'logic' were proving futile. I was communicating on the wrong level. This wasn't a factual argument, weighing up the pros and cons of alternative ways forward; this was about emotions. All my efforts to appeal to my wife's brain were of no use. I needed to aim for her heart but someone else already had that. With a steadily building sense of frustration, sadness and fear, I realised that I wasn't going to be able to change her mind—a 'solid', 'practical' marriage is no competition for a love affair.

*

Unfortunately, there was even more than this calamitous event going on in my life and the other thing was right up there on the emotional pain meter as well. Five months earlier my father, who lived in the UK along with the rest of my family, had been diagnosed with an aggressive form of pancreatic cancer. Typical life expectancy for this vicious form of cancer is six months from the time of diagnosis and so my poor old dad was about to enter the 'living on borrowed time' phase.

Two weeks after the discovery of my wife's infidelity, I made the long trip back to the UK to spend some time with him, swapping one emotional nightmare for another. It was awful. I endured a week with my parents watching my father struggling to fight the cancer and trying to keep positive about his outlook, when all the statistics indicated that, for a seventy-one-year-old man, the chances of survival were just a little bit better than zero. It was the last time that I would be with him when he was conscious, although I didn't know it at the time, and there was so much I wanted to talk to him about. But I couldn't find the words because I was so distracted by what was happening in my own life.

We drove around the country visiting healers; we played cards; and we spent time as a family. My mum, my dad, my brother, my sister and me—a family unit, just as we had been twenty-five years earlier. We hadn't been together like this, without the distraction of our own families, for years. It was a bitter-sweet time and an opportunity to simply exist with each other, but I was consumed by the thought that I was part of two family units, and they were both breaking up. Too much of my world was changing at the same time and, to this day, I still feel cheated that I was unable to fully focus on my dad during his final few weeks of life.

I desperately wanted to tell these four people closest to me about my situation. I needed to talk about it and share my pain but my family was suffering enough and it didn't seem right. My mum, brother and sister were all concentrating on Dad, sharing his struggle and hoping against hope that he would prove to be the one who, with positive thought and effective chemo, would beat the odds and survive this awful disease.

I lived, for a while, in the familiarity of my old house with my parents, surrounded by the trappings of a happy family life and a successful marriage. My brilliant mum and dad. Had I been lured into a false sense of security? Because their marriage was so good and looked so easy had I taken my eye off the ball—thinking that's how all marriages are?

We sat on the sofa, eating homemade scones and drinking tea. All normal. Except that it wasn't normal. My dad had a cancer growing inside him and I had my own personal cancer growing inside me. I wanted to blurt out "I hate to burden you at this difficult time but my marriage is over". I kept it in. I wanted my dad to go to his grave thinking that I had a happy marriage and that my move to Australia had been worthwhile. My wife and I had already agreed that we wouldn't tell the children about the forthcoming split, and we wouldn't separate, until my dad had passed away. His ability to cling onto life would determine how much longer my own family had left.

2

Leaving me now

The mental pain of separation is tough enough but, as a special bonus, you also get some interesting physical side effects thrown in for free. I couldn't sleep properly, I couldn't eat properly, my heart rate was up, my blood pressure was up, I was angry, I was frustrated, I was sad and my eyes would occasionally well-up on the train to and from work. Annoyingly, everyone else on the train seemed happy and relaxed, iPods in their ears, reading the paper or just dozing. I wasn't relaxed and I wasn't happy. I wanted to tell the whole train what was going on in my life and that my wife was behaving like an idiot, but as an Englishman it has been ingrained in me that public scenes of emotion are just not on. I have been brought up to believe that worse things happen at sea. Personal tragedy is just one of those things that is best ignored—everything can be solved by a nice cup of tea.

I took to wearing my shades on the train—regardless of the weather or the time of day. Far better to walk into a piece of train furniture and injure myself, than to run the risk of people seeing my tears. One evening at Flinders Street station a kind little old lady asked me if I needed any help getting onto the train. I felt a bit bad about this but realised that, if I got onto the train with my arms outstretched, complemented by a zombie-style walk—or the kind of walk required after being hit in the nuts by Brett Lee—then someone would direct me to the special seat near the doors and make sure I was comfy. My dark glasses routine meant that I would never need to stand on a peak hour train again. We English are right—every cloud does have a silver lining.

So, during the final few months of 'living' with my wife (well, we were technically living together but we weren't actually together), I changed physically. I thought I had lost a little bit of weight because I could get both my hands down the front of my trousers—it was like being thirteen again—but I wasn't aware quite how much I had lost until I had a fitness assessment in the gym. This was a six monthly event that required riding a bike for twelve minutes while my blood pressure was measured (it had gone up quite dramatically), trying to touch my toes and do a full sit-up (I failed, but I don't think I can blame that on separation stress) and performing various other activities which involved grunting, prodding and measuring. At the end of the session my instructor weighed me. I watched her go to my file to write down my new weight and look up surprised, before asking me to get back on the scales again. I am not a big guy and my weight had dropped from 73kg to 68kg—that's an impressive weight loss of 6.8 per cent in *Biggest Loser* speak. I had also adopted the gaunt look. Heroin chic, here we come!

I was a bit disappointed that on my trip home to see my dad none of my family had noticed my spectacular weight loss and generally thin disposition. I was sure someone would either enquire about my new fitness regime or else ask whether I was feeling all right. Still, I suppose there were other things on their minds, and my dad was completely outdoing me in the weight loss and gauntness stakes. Compared to him, I looked good.

Meanwhile, my wife and I continued to put on a brave face

for the children. We still hadn't told them what was going on and had agreed it was important that life appeared to be normal, although I had become very dark and withdrawn. My wife took to sleeping in the spare room on the basis that she was "seeing someone else" and it would be "inappropriate for me to see her naked". Weird—I knew every inch of her body intimately, and now it belonged to someone else and was off limits. Our cover story was that I still had jet lag from my trip to the UK and I was keeping her awake. But children aren't stupid and they knew something was up, although they didn't say anything at the time. They later told me that they thought it was me who wanted to leave the marriage, as I was the one who appeared to be unhappy!

In a vain attempt to make our last months together as bearable as possible, we introduced a few rules. My wife promised not to see her soul mate again until we had formally separated and were living apart. I promised not to discuss our 'difficulties'—a word that I found, even as an Englishman, to be a bit of an understatement—with anyone else. I wasn't 100 per cent convinced she was sticking to her end of the bargain. I once came home from work to find her in the shower (due to the 'inappropriate' ruling I didn't try and see her naked), only for her to appear moments later in her exercise gear. She announced that she was off to the gym—the scene of the crime—and I suggested, completely logically in my view, that it seemed a bit pointless having a shower before she went. She told me, with a straight face, that she didn't want to get there feeling sweaty. (Get where? I thought). It was ridiculous. I was worried that my wife, who had cheated on me and decided to leave me, was cheating on me.

Looking back, it seems stupid that I tried so hard to hold on to our marriage, but in my mind we had, seemingly overnight, gone from being happy to my wife wanting to be with someone else. It took a bit of getting used to.

A month later I was back in the UK. I had a call from my brother one Saturday morning. I was lying in bed, alone of course, hungover after a big night out with the boys—drinking was the one thing that seemed to come more and more easily to me. My brother told me that my dad was getting weaker very quickly and that I needed to get back there as soon as I could.

The prognosis didn't sound good. They had made up a bed for him downstairs, he wasn't eating or drinking, had pretty much stopped talking and a 24-hour nurse had arrived. That afternoon I was back on the plane again. It's a long trip to the UK and it couldn't go fast enough, I didn't want to land at Heathrow to get a message that I was too late. But I needn't have worried, my dad was a fighter and he waited for me. I arrived home just in time for his last two days.

My entire family—my mum, my brother and my sister—met me at the front door to my parents' house. They looked worried for me. They had seen my dad's day-by-day deterioration over the previous two weeks. They had seen his metamorphosis from a man who was thin and gaunt, but essentially alive, to a man who was now bedridden, doped up on painkillers and with very little life left in him. I had been spared watching his life decaying away and they wanted to prepare me for what was waiting for me in the next room. They wanted me to be ready for what I was about to experience.

But who can prepare you for this? I walked into the room and there he was. My dad, the protector of our family, the man who had been my father for all of my life, humbled by this hideous, unrelenting cancer. I wasn't prepared for this at all. How could I have been prepared to see the man who had been so strong and such an important part of my world, so helpless? How could anyone be prepared for that?

My dad made a feeble attempt, which I didn't even notice, to sit up in bed but the effort overwhelmed him. All he could do was turn his head and look at me through half-closed eyes and whisper something I couldn't hear. And that was it. I held his hand and he drifted back into his final coma.

I spent the rest of the day sitting with him, watching him, listening to his breathing. We would wet his lips and his tongue would flick out, desperate for the moisture. But eventually even that little movement stopped. At one point during our vigil my brother and I helped the nurse to clean him up after he soiled himself and, as we turned him, he grabbed our arms tightly and his eyes opened with a look of fear and bewilderment. He had become a baby again, his actions driven only by reflexes, stripped of all his dignity.

I was tired that night, the jet lag and emotion had kicked in and I needed to sleep. I spent a few minutes with my dad, squeezed his hand, told him that I loved him and that we would be all right without him, and said my last goodnight. I fully expected to wake up the next day to find him gone.

But having woken early the following morning, I went downstairs and, to my surprise, found that my dad was still with us. Still lying there, still breathing quietly. But during the day his breathing became softer and shallower and his reflex movements fewer and fewer, until eventually his body gave up. My dad died peacefully, his family around his bedside, on a wonderful, calm summer's evening, the sun just starting to dip below the horizon while casting a gentle light over the big oak tree in his garden. It was a beautiful time and a beautiful place to die. As he slipped away I was hit by a towering wave of grief. My feelings of sorrow and loss for my dad were compounded by the even greater sorrow and fear over what was to become of my own family when I got back to Australia. This was much too much to grieve over. How much pain can one heart take?

It would be a week before the funeral. A week when reality seemed to stop and our lives were put on hold. My dad was dead but not yet buried and my marriage was terminally ill but not yet dead. I stayed with my mum and we waited. We waited for the ceremony that would tell us that the time had come for us to move on with our lives. For my mum, brother and sister that would mean learning to live without my dad. For me it would mean so much more. My dad would be buried and my marriage would soon be dead.

The funeral was painful and, when it was over, I didn't want to go home. I felt as though I could suspend reality by staying longer in the UK. But, of course, that was impossible, and two days later I was off and heading back to Australia. It was a long, lonely trip home—and this time I wanted it to take forever.

Now that my father had passed away, the day of reckoning for my own family had arrived. My wife insisted that the children had to be told—she needed to move on. I wasn't sure whether, when the moment came, she would be able to go through with it and hoped this might be the one thing that would keep us together. Surely she wouldn't be able to hurt the children, wouldn't be able to turn their lives on their heads and we would survive as a family—wouldn't we? I was wrong again. A happy family life is no competition for a love affair.

The plan was for us to tell them together but I couldn't do it. I don't know whether I was being a coward or shirking my responsibilities, but I didn't want to be there at the death of my family. I had just been through a traumatic family death and I was in no state to cope with another one. My wife called the girls down from upstairs and I went out into the garden while she prepared to bring our family life to a close.

I sat there looking back at the house and looking back on all the wonderful times we had enjoyed as a family. We were a great family—we worked well together, we laughed, the children were happy and we had fun—surely it wasn't all going to come to an end? Again, I wondered whether my wife would have the strength to go through with it. In these final moments, would she be able to tell our girls the words that every child dreads, the words that my eldest had told me she was pleased she would never hear because we were such a strong family? When I could stand the tension no longer I came back into the house, hoping that there may have been a change of heart. But there was nothing but silence, broken only by the sobbing of my family—my wife and my fourteen- and twelve-year-old daughters.

It was all over.

Bollocks. Big, bastard, hairy, baboon-sized bollocks.

3

And then there were three

So it was done, our time together as a family had come to a close and there was no going back. We got down to the mechanics. How would the split work and when, my wife politely enquired, would I be moving out? Me move out? What?

"It's traditional in these situations that the father moves out so the mother can look after the children," she pontificated.

She sounded like a lawyer or a judge, so matter of fact, hardnosed and sure of herself.

"Really," I replied. "I thought it was traditional for a husband and wife to stay married—for richer for poorer, for better for worse and all that good stuff."

God, I could be annoying—but I was pissed off that she was being so heartless. And why should I be the one to look for somewhere new to live? She wanted to leave me. Why did that mean I had to be the one doing the moving out?

"It's typical of you to take such a traditional view of marriage," she replied.

I was confused. I wasn't sure what was traditional anymore. Was it traditional to stay together or to break up? Did the fact that so many marriages fail mean this was now an expectation—that splitting up was the new normal?

Anyway, no time for philosophy, I needed to take guard quickly because Brett Lee was on his mark and getting ready to deliver another bouncer. And it was a ripper. My wife had decided that I would move out of our house from Monday to Friday, but move back in again at the weekends. This would have the benefit of allowing her to look after the children during the week, her 'traditional' role, while also allowing her the freedom to "explore her relationship" with her soul mate at the weekends—a less 'traditional' role in my view. Or put another way, I would be free from household distractions during the week to enable me to concentrate on work and earning the money to keep the wheels turning, my 'traditional' role, while she would be free to spend the weekends as she pleased—out on the town, going away or rooting like a rabbit with her soul mate. I imagined that this arrangement would condemn me to hard weekends of running the children around and lonely midweek evenings of TV.

Incredibly, my wife had even found an apartment for me to rent just around the corner from our house. "You will be very happy in it and not too far away," she told me. She always knew what was best for me. And how comforting that she was prepared to be so considerate and supportive in my hour of need.

I was horrified. How much of this had she, or worse, they planned? Would her soul mate also be moving in with her when I moved out during the week, so they could be together? Would he be perusing my CD collection—"Ah, *Ready 'n' Willing*, the classic Whitesnake album of the late 70s. Your old man has got taste". What if he forgot his clean undies? Would he think about borrowing a pair of mine? (Obviously they would be far too big for him). Would he sit in bed reading the newspaper in the morning, having a cup of tea, while wearing my dressing gown? Or would he bring his own dressing gown, and leave it hanging behind the bathroom door over the weekend—a permanent reminder of his presence—so that it was ready for him the following week? Would I come home to find a photo of his kids on my bedside table? More appallingly, would he try and take over my role as father—would he make friends with my girls, help them with their homework, make them laugh, dazzle them with his Origami and shadow puppeting skills and take them out for Chinese? All these hideous visions went through my head and seemed to dwarf the more realistic and equally appalling fact, that the main thing he would be doing if he came to stay was boning my wife.

But back to Brett Lee. It was a good ball—short, fast and snorting off the pitch. But no more Gladstone Small, timid tailender, for me. I rocked back on my heels and hit it clean over the boundary. I became Allan Lamb (he is sort of English after all). The look on the cover fielders' faces as it sailed over their heads was priceless.

"I'm not moving out," I said. "If you want to be with this guy that's up to you—but I'm going nowhere."

It was one of the best decisions I ever made. Much later my lawyer told me that the first thing she asks her clients is "have you moved out?" hoping they haven't. For most men it's too late. They do the 'traditional' thing, pack their bags and move into an apartment. Here's a top tip for men going through separation—if you are able to stay put in your own home, then do it. The person living in the family home holds all the aces in the tough months of negotiations and arguments to come.

So the die was cast and the big decisions made. My wife had decided, because I was being so unreasonable about the living arrangements (i.e. not doing what she wanted me to), that she would be the one to move out and that she and her soul mate would find somewhere new to live so that they could be together. How lovely for them! This made things a lot easier for my daughters. They chose to live with me. They were unhappy and angry with their mother for the pain that she had caused us all and were ashamed of the nature of her affair—and they certainly weren't interested in living with some guy who they hadn't met and had no intention of meeting. Being able to stay in their familiar home and surroundings with me, when so much of their world was changing, was the best outcome for them and the best outcome for me.

Time raced by and a few weeks later the September school holidays were upon us. Months before, in the time before separation which now felt like years ago, we had planned to go back to England during these holidays as a family to see my father. He didn't live that long, but the children and I decided we would go anyway; they needed a change of scene and I needed to spend some time with my UK family now that they knew what had happened. I needed some family support. But it would be another bitter-sweet moment—this trip would mark the end of our own time as a family unit. My wife would move out while we were away.

My wife drove us to the airport and we said our final goodbyes at the Singapore Airlines check-in desk. Lots of other people around us were also saying their goodbyes—ours were just a little more final. Sophie, Annabel and I were, officially, a threesome. It was a massive, life changing moment and yet I couldn't stop thinking of the Genesis album *And Then There Were Three* and the beginning of the track *Many Too Many* which kept coming into my head—"Many too many have stood where I stand, many more will stand here too". Fortunately the vision of Phil Collins proved to be only fleeting and passed once we were on the plane. It was going to be a long, hard flight to London and I didn't need Phil with me every step of the way.

As many people know, flying with children can be challenging—but it is much more so in my case. My youngest daughter has a fear of the claustrophobia brought about by long haul flying, which is a little inconvenient when I have family on the other side of the world. It means that, at some point in the flight, she will start being sick and then continue in this vein at regular intervals until the end of the journey—at which point a bottle of Gatorade will result in an immediate and miraculous recovery. As she has got older, the onset of the air sickness has been delayed and, on our last trip from the UK a few years earlier, she actually managed to get halfway to Singapore before filling my shoes with chicken or fish (it was hard to tell which it was when it was on the meal tray—and even harder to tell once it had been regurgitated).

We boarded the plane, gently clunked the heads of a few of our fellow passengers with our rather generous volume of hand luggage, and took our seats. I sat in-between the girls in the row of three seats, which would be home for the next twenty-four hours. Tonight's trip would be my third in four months to the UK and I had become something of an expert in economy class sleeping. This new found ability was not the result of any significant scientific research or analysis, it was simply that I got off my trolley by speed drinking several glasses of wine and passing on dinner. Sleep was then an inevitable consequence. I was pretty sure that my daughter would make it to Singapore in one piece and, in any case, she would wake me up if she felt sick.

Hours later I woke in a slight panic from a dream, in which I had been hog-tied and put in a sack by some strange cowboy, hillbilly type characters, to find that I couldn't move. I swear I could hear the sound of a banjo being tuned up. However, as my eyes groggily opened, I realised that everything was okay—I had just fallen asleep with my head on the tray table and as a result my back and neck had gone into spasm. I half lay and half sat, bent over the tray table, paralysed but with my eyes open and with a little pool of dribble forming under my cheek. As I remained in my inert state, willing my body back to life, the woman sitting across the aisle caught my eye.

"Your daughter's been sick," she growled, looking at me in disgust.

She was right. The poor thing had started her vomiting only forty-five minutes into the flight and had spent the last five hours regularly puking into a sick bag and then going to the toilet to clean up. She didn't want to wake me and, unfortunately, my well-practiced economy class sleep routine had ensured that I was oblivious to her distress. In hindsight it was fairly obvious that the stress brought on by our final goodbyes at the airport, combined with her fear of flying, was likely to cause her vomiting to start much earlier into the flight than normal. But at the time, her 'caring' father, who had not really thought this through, was 'un-contactable' in the grip of an alcohol-induced coma.

I maintained unpleasant eye contact with the woman across the aisle, my head still stuck on the tray table, trying to work out how I could get my body to straighten while hunched up in the cramped seat. She continued to stare at me no doubt assuming, perhaps correctly, that I was some drunken, pathetic, incompetent father. I finally managed to rouse myself, gasping in pain, and somehow achieved the feat of standing up while doing a fairly good impression of Quasimodo. Great start to my new life, I thought to myself.

Our holiday in the UK was a very emotional time for all of us. My dad wasn't there, and for the girls their mum wasn't there. But at least the conflict and tension that had blighted our last month wasn't there either. It was a great environment for me to start bonding with my daughters. For the first time ever I was responsible for them twenty-four hours a day. We didn't talk much about what we had been through or what was to come, we treated it as a holiday. I was amazed how happy my girls seemed. Sophie, my eldest, was, unusually, a little bit clingy. She became slightly anxious when I left her and Annabel at my sister's house for a night while I went to my mum's house to go through my dad's financial affairs. She wanted to know how long I would be gone and when I would get back, and she called me a couple of times to make sure that everything was alright. Other than that, life seemed quite normal. Or perhaps it was just the calm before the storm.

When we got back to Australia three weeks later there was no one at the airport to meet us. The three of us stood waiting for a cab in the dark, rainy Melbourne morning. It was a quiet journey back to the house. Each of us was tired and lost in our own thoughts about the reality we would face when we got home and how our new lives were going to turn out. I was wondering how I would cope as a single father—and I have no doubt that the girls were thinking the same thing. I also had the vain hope my wife might have changed her mind and would be waiting for us at home and, again, I was sure that the girls were quietly hoping the same thing.

An hour later we pulled into the driveway. The house was dark and quiet. It didn't look as though anyone was home. I went into the bedroom and opened the wardrobes. It seemed impossible, but they were empty. Her clothes were gone. She had moved out. It was the beginning of my new life as a single dad.

I was happy my children had chosen to live with me, rather than my wife. I didn't want to miss out on living with my daughters and their growing up just because my wife had decided that she wanted to live with someone else. And I wasn't going to take the—supposedly—easy way out and become a weekend father. I was determined to fulfil my responsibilities to my children. It was what I wanted. There was just one small problem—I didn't know how I was going to do it.

I would need to learn fast.

4

Welcome to the jungle

Saturday morning. My first weekend as a single father had arrived. I woke up on my own, collected the newspaper from the end of the driveway, fed the dogs, made a cup of tea and got back into bed. On a 'normal' Saturday I would have followed this routine with my wife and we would have talked about our plans for the weekend. She was the weekend organiser so, in reality, it would typically have been a case of her telling me what she had planned.

As I finished my cup of tea I realised that I didn't actually have any plans. I wasn't going anywhere on Saturday night and I didn't have anyone dropping round over the weekend. This didn't worry me. I am not an unduly sociable person so I thought a quiet weekend would be quite nice and would give me the chance to record some overnight Premier League soccer to watch at my convenience on Sunday. No more trying to squeeze my own interests into a busy weekend, there would be plenty of 'me time' I thought (rather naively as it turned out). More evidence that a good cup of tea does, in fact, make everything seem better.

I started a mental list of the things that I vaguely imagined I would need to do over the weekend.

Firstly, I had to get the girls to and from dance. That was straightforward as it had been my responsibility on most weekends.

Sophie would probably be going to a 'gathering' in the evening. I should briefly explain the three key forms of weekend entertainment available to twelve- to fourteen-year-olds for the benefit of those without teenage children. Apparently these are formal definitions and will shortly appear in all good dictionaries:

1. *Having friends over (verb—passive)*: involves less than ten kids; no loud music, alcohol or making out. The preferred option of parents.
2. *Gathering (noun):* one step up from having friends over but one step down from a party; involves ten to twenty kids; maybe some dancing; potential for limited amounts of smuggled alcohol; opportunities for making out—but this is generally frowned upon.
3. *Party (verb—active)*: more than thirty kids; definitely dancing; potential for officially provided alcohol; most likely making out. High stress event—a parent's nightmare.

But, regardless of the specifics of the event, I normally did the weekend evening running around so that should be manageable as well. So far so good. My mental list got longer:

1. The lawn needed mowing. I was used to doing that every couple of weeks so I should be able to fit it in. It would require an hour or so.
2. The dogs needed to be walked. They hadn't been exercised all week so it had to be done. This used to be a shared responsibility, which was now exclusively mine, and would require around forty-five minutes.

3. I would need to make dinner. Not sure exactly what that involved as it wasn't my domain. I decided to allow thirty to forty five minutes for cooking and cleaning up.
4. Making dinner meant getting some food. I dimly recalled that my wife used to go to the fruit shop during the week. This was completely new territory for me, but I would need to fit it in today because I was short of fruit and veg. Then probably a stop at the butcher to get some meat. Again, not too bad, as they were both just up the road so I could probably manage that in between the afternoon dance runs.
5. Mustn't forget the washing and ironing. I would need to get my work shirts done. I used to do the ironing when I was originally single. It was a boring job but do-able. Maybe I could iron them while I watched the soccer? Sunday job—allow thirty minutes.
6. Thinking about washing—did the kids have things that needed to be washed and ironed? School dresses and blouses? How many had they got and did they wear a clean one each day (if they did they wouldn't for much longer). What about bed sheets? When was the last time mine were washed? And did I need to wash them if I was the only one in them? I had a quick look. They appeared to be clean and so I felt they could skip a wash.
7. Speaking of cleaning—did I need to clean the house this weekend? Vacuuming I could do, but what about the toilets, sinks, bath and kitchen? Was that a weekly thing? Did it take long?

My mental list was quite daunting and I was starting to feel a little bit depressed. My cup of tea had gone cold and I didn't think another one would suddenly make everything seem better. I looked at the clock—it was 8.30am. I reckoned that if I had got up at 6.30am I might have had a chance of getting everything done. Fortunately, my management consulting training kicked in—what I needed was a plan—and I also thought that dividing the day into thirds would be helpful. My plan went something like this:

Morning—put washing on; vacuum; walk dogs. Home for coffee by 11 o'clock—read the paper for a bit and relax.

Afternoon—dance drop off; fruit shop; butcher; dance pick up.

Evening—make dinner; deliver girls to social event(s) as required; glass of wine (hold back because I'm driving); bit of TV; collect girls from social event(s) as required. Bed.

That left lawn mowing, cleaning, ironing and a potential second dog walk for Sunday.

Unfortunately, my plan had the unintended consequence of making me even more depressed. It wasn't really the recipe for a great weekend. But anyway, there was no time to waste. I managed to get the washing on and start the vacuuming. Sophie appeared and made breakfast—and a mess. Cereals and margarine left out, bowl and plate on top of the dishwasher but not in it.

"Can you put your things in the dishwasher?" I shouted over the vacuum cleaner.

"I can't because it's full of clean stuff," she replied, as she disappeared back upstairs to the pleasures of Facebook.

And should I have been surprised? The girls had never been responsible for chores before, after all, they had been used to having two parents to keep the house running. I didn't want to be too tough on day one, so I stopped vacuuming to unstack the dishwasher in the vain hope that it might result in the girls putting their dirty dishes in it—it made no difference initially, but we got there in the end.

Back to the vacuuming. Annabel appeared.

"Dad, I need to get some new ballet shoes before dance this afternoon."

"Okay, after I've finished the vacuuming," I said. "Don't forget to put your dirty stuff in the dishwasher."

It sounded more like a plea than a firm instruction.

Time check: 10.30am. According to my plan I was supposed to be back from the dog walk by 11 o'clock and having a coffee. In reality I was way behind schedule and starting to feel a bit stressed.

But, again, no time to waste, we jumped in the car and set off to Camberwell to get the ballet shoes. Do you know what Saturday traffic is like? It's a disaster—and finding somewhere to park was a nightmare. I was continually out-foxed by little old ladies. I would drive round and round looking for a parking space, while they would slowly follow someone who was walking along carrying shopping bags until they got to their car, and then sit blocking off the lane with their indicator flashing. But, eventually, I found a space—joy! Looked at the sign—P10 and not 2P—bollocks! Ten minutes—we would have to run.

Got the shoes. Annabel wanted a Boost juice on the way back to the car. No time. Let's go. Argument. Stress. Why are kids so unreasonable? Please don't cry. I stopped in my tracks. Who was being unreasonable here? It was me. The poor girl was going through the trauma of a family break-up for God's sake, was no doubt missing her mother, and I was being an unreasonable parent by rushing her back to the car when what she needed was some time out with a Boost. It wasn't all about me and my schedule.

So we both got a Boost and, rather than running back to the car, sat on a bench to drink them. Maybe I would get a parking ticket, but it was more important right now to spend some time with my daughter. I apologised to her for being so mean. I explained that I had to learn how to run the house properly, that it was going to be hard work until I got used to it and, if I got cranky, it would be because I was frustrated with myself, and not because I was cross with her or her sister. She didn't say much apart from "I love you Dad". I felt my heart break and wished that I had my shades with me because I could feel my eyes welling up (and I can still feel the tears all these years later as I write this).

We walked back to the car hand-in-hand. This had been the first real conversation I'd had with my daughter for a long time. It wasn't just my world that had been turned on its head—her world was also on its head. What she needed most of all was not a clean house and a nicely mown lawn, but some time with me where we could talk or just sit together sharing a Boost. Come to think of it, that was what I needed too. As we walked I resolved that the girls would come first, before anything else, and that my prime purpose as a father would be to make sure they had as normal and as happy a childhood as I could possibly give them. It put everything into perspective—and I didn't even get a parking ticket. I took this as a sign that God was on my side.

Back home. Time check: Lunchtime. Where had the morning gone? Rethink required. The three of us had lunch together. I couldn't remember the last time we had done this, and it was fun. We made toasted sandwiches, trying to outdo each other with the number of fillings we could fit in and the most imaginative mess that we could make. The girls even put their dirty plates in the dishwasher, unfortunately in a slightly disorganised way that required some significant re-packing, but it was a start.

A quick cup of tea and I was ready for the big afternoon push. I loaded the entire family of girls and dogs into the car; dropped off the two-legged members at dance; walked the four-legged members in the park; got back home; checked the fridge and set off to the fruit shop and butcher. Very efficient. I rewarded myself with a small, Tim Henman-esq, fist pump.

"You miserable, lazy bastard," I heard myself muttering, not loudly but not quietly enough. I was standing outside the butcher's shop looking at his sign that informed me that his Saturday opening hours were 8.30am to 12.30pm. Why? Did he think that he was doing the community a favour by sacrificing part of his weekend and deigning to open on a Saturday morning? What about all the poor sods who only got the chance to do their shopping at the weekend? This was Saturday afternoon, peak time—why not think of the customer and close on Monday instead, you selfish bugger?

Down the street to the fruit shop. Same story. Shutters drawn, no official opening hours displayed, but obviously the greengrocer had had enough of today as well and was probably now having a nice sit down and a well-earned beer with the butcher.

A little old lady walked past me towing a fat Corgi. She had obviously overheard my muttering about the selfishness of my local purveyors of fresh meat and vegetables and gave me a look that seemed to say "young people today". For a moment I actually thought I was going to have a major melt down and apply my right foot to the rear end of her waddling pooch.

But there was no point taking out my frustration on a geriatric dog or its geriatric owner, I had work to do, and besides, I had two dogs that I could kick later in the privacy of my own home if I needed to. There was an hour before dance pick up. Could I get to Coles, shop, unpack and be at dance within an hour?

It would be tight, but if I didn't go now there was a real danger that I was going to run into dinnertime.

Back in the car and off to Coles. Saturday afternoon shopping is very different to the late night or Sunday morning dashes to pick up some milk or bread that I was used to. Normally it's easy to park at Coles—but not on a Saturday afternoon. Round and round I went looking for a space. Level 1, then Level 2, then Level 3—still no success. Time was running short. I was incapable of rational thought. Why did all these people have to shop now? Should the Government force people to shop in their own suburb? Why didn't Coles have executive parking as they do at the airport? Why did people dawdle so much?

My frenzied thinking was interrupted by my sudden emergence from the darkness into the light, not metaphorically but literally, the top floor of the car park was in the open. I had never been this far up in the car park before and I was temporarily in awe of my discovery—wait 'til I tell my friends about this, I thought.

Unfortunately, my brief moment of wonder was shattered by the realisation that the downside of being on the top of the car park was being further from the actual shop itself. I ran to the lift and pressed the button. A little old lady smiled at me. I pressed the button a few more times on the basis that this would make the lift come more quickly. The little old lady smiled at me again. Still no lift. Bugger it, I thought—time for the stairs. Down I ran. I was quite impressed by my ability to keep up a good pace and dodge all of the dawdlers who were making their way both up and down. Did they think I had lost it? Had I lost it? After all, I only needed to get some weekend groceries; it wasn't a life-threatening event. I would have to do this on a regular basis so I couldn't continue with the stress of my own version of extreme shopping forever.

Out of the stairwell. Dodged a few people studying lettuces at the market stall and on to Coles. At that moment I knew that, if I hadn't lost it before, then I had now—officially—lost it. As I saw the neatly lined up shopping trolleys, I was certain that my chances of having a $1 or $2 coin to secure the release of one of their number were slim. I hate this system. We don't have it in England and I was often caught out and annoyed by it in Australia, even when I was in a good mood. It doesn't make any sense to me. Does it really stop drunken students from using a trolley to get one of their fallen comrades home after a hard night of active service? I knew that I didn't have any change and I also knew that I didn't really have time to go shopping anyway.

I felt tired and useless. The failure to get any shopping suddenly felt like a symbol for my failed life and took on a significance out of all proportion. Standing outside Coles I felt totally alone, and the despair of my situation washed over me. I felt like giving up. I hung my head, took a deep sigh and turned to go back to my car.

As I looked up, the little old lady from the roof top car park passed me, dragging her personal shopping trolley. She smiled at me. It was a sad smile, not like the look I'd received from the previous little old lady with her corgi outside the fruit shop. I smiled back. She knew that I knew, that she knew, that I was a tosser. I imagined that she was a widow, struggling with the recent loss of her husband, the onset of old age and the deterioration of her body. Life was probably hard for her yet she was still smiling, and it looked as though she was coping better than I was. I had to do better. If she could do it then I could do it—thank you, you inspirational little old lady! I went home for a nice cup of tea. I even managed a smile when I was charged a dollar for my five-minute use of the car park.

By the time I had picked up the girls from dance and got back home I was in no mood for a return trip to Coles. Shopping would have to be added to the Sunday list, along with the lawn mowing, cleaning, ironing and potential dog walk. Wasn't Sunday supposed to be the day of rest?

The girls were hungry and it was now time for dinner, but because of my shopping failures the menu choices were a little limited. I remembered my wife used to knock up a tuna and pasta combination as a meal of last resort when she was back late from the gym or 'somewhere'. I didn't really want to think about the gym or the 'somewhere' but at least the memory had given me an idea for dinner. I wasn't sure of the specifics but I reckoned that if I cooked some pasta, opened a tin of tuna and stuck the contents on top, I would be 80 per cent of the way there. Fifteen minutes later it was done. It didn't look too flash to be fair but, fortunately, I had a creative *MasterChef*-style brainwave and added some grated cheese to the mix. Although this didn't do too much for the presentation, at least it added an additional food group to the concoction.

Dinner was served! On the one hand I felt good that I was providing nourishment for my children, but on the other, I recognised that the combination of warm pasta topped with cold tuna and cheese did not make for a great meal. The girls said how much they enjoyed it—bless them. One even went beyond the call of duty and further demonstrated her enjoyment by having a second helping. But the sad truth was that my wife's meal of last resort had become my Saturday night signature dish. I added cooking to the list of things that I needed to do better.

However, there was a glimmer of good news as far as the evening was concerned. Neither of the girls were going out, instead one of them was having a friend over. This gave me the opportunity to either catch up on some of my chores, or have a glass or two of wine. It had been a hard day so I went for the alcohol option. With the girls happy upstairs, I made myself comfy, poured a generous glass of red and thought back on the day. If I was going to survive I needed to manage my household chores far more efficiently. I realised two things. One, that I hadn't given my wife enough credit for running the house while she too was working full-time, and the other that I was going to have to earn my leisure time. 'Me time' would be a reward for efficiency.

5

Sunday bloody Sunday

Sunday morning. Same start as Saturday, a cup of tea and the paper in bed, but I wasn't as relaxed as I had been the previous morning, I had more work to do and the clock was ticking. I decided to go to Coles early. A piece of male advice I had been given, and which I thought might be quite positive, was that supermarkets are the new nightclubs for the 40-plus generation, full of lonely, single women and a great place to pick up.

I wondered whether the supermarket world was similar to the nightclub world, although this was a difficult concept for me to analyse fully as I rarely went to the supermarket, and I couldn't even remember the last time I had been to a nightclub. Did different supermarkets attract a different type of punter? Did Coles have a higher social standing than Safeway, with a more sophisticated clientele? Did location make a difference— would supermarkets nearer the city be more expensive and harder to get into? Were some supermarkets meat markets? Obviously they are all meat markets to a degree, but you know what I'm getting at. Would there be security whose job was to turn away large groups of men, or those people who didn't have the 'right look'? Would I need to wear a collar and proper shoes?

A lot to think about over my Sunday morning cornflakes.

I wasn't really looking to pick up but, on the basis that my local Coles might become my new local wine bar and first impressions could be important, I thought I should at least make an effort on my initial visit. I went for a pair of jeans and a relatively trendy shirt, a sort of 'happening' single dad look.

I was slightly apprehensive as I went through the doors to Coles. I was nervous about all the new people that I was about to meet and wondered whether, in an hour or two, I would be sharing a flat white with my new, fabulously exciting, friends. Given the build up to my trip, and the agonising over which shirt gave me the best enigmatic and interesting, yet available, look, it was a bit disappointing to realise that, in reality, Coles at 10 o'clock on a Sunday morning is actually just a supermarket.

It has to be said that there were quite a lot of 40-plus singles in the house, but they were mostly fairly sad looking blokes. Even in the early days of my new life I could easily recognise the single men. Their trolleys were a giveaway—baked beans, cup-a-soups, frozen chips, frozen pies, ready meals (single serve) and so on—all the hallmarks of a solitary life. It occurred to me that the reason sales of Lean Cuisine meals have risen so dramatically recently is not because women are buying them as part of a calorie controlled diet, but because you can chuck them in the microwave. They have become a key part of the single man's diet and volumes are up because men need to eat three of them at a time to feel full.

There were also a few women in the store but they didn't appear to be treating their shopping trip as a pseudo nightclub experience. In fact it was the complete opposite. The women had generally adopted a grim faced, determined look as though the trip to Coles was a necessary evil and they were attempting to break their individual course record for a weekly shop. They were dressed for it too. A tracksuit is clearly the fashion choice of the efficient female shopper. There was no interaction, no flirty looks, no sexual tension—the only occasional moments of excitement and whispered gasps seemed to be caused by the discovery of a new weekly special.

After spending thirty minutes taking in the Coles vibe and concluding that this would not form a key plank of my future social life, I realised, rather disappointingly, that my trolley only contained some milk and a small packet of cheese slices. My lack of progress was due to a combination of factors—partly the distraction of my social observations, partly because I didn't know where anything was and, perhaps most importantly, the fact that I didn't have a list and therefore didn't know what I needed to buy. But I did need to get going so, to speed things up, I took what I considered to be a fairly practical route and, starting at the first aisle, went through the whole store putting in two of every item I thought I might need for my new life, a sort of Noah's ark approach to shopping.

It's amazing what you can buy in a supermarket. There is so much more to it than just food—cleaning products, batteries, insect repellent, printer cartridges, Christmas crackers on special, Easter eggs on special, Halloween gear on special. I was like the proverbial kid in a candy store and within an hour I had a fully loaded trolley. It was a bit of a shock at the checkout.

"That will be $408.57," said Sharni.

"Oh okay." Bloody hell—was that a lot? Still, I reckoned I had a month's supply of food in my trolley.

"Have a relaxing afternoon," she said, in what I thought was a slightly ambiguous way.

Was she suggesting something else? I hesitated as I pretended to study my receipt, playing for time. What was the etiquette here? Was there more to come? Was she expecting me to make a move?

"You need to move your stuff," she barked.

"Oh okay. Sorry."

I guess I was wrong. And anyway, why would a nineteen-year-old check-out chick be interested in a middle aged bloke who couldn't even get his groceries into his trolley efficiently? I saw her eyes roll as she greeted the next customer. I couldn't leave quickly enough.

I got home feeling good about my newly successful hunter-gatherer role. The floor was strewn with my shopping. The girls came down—hyenas around the kill—and started going through the bags.

"Did you get any BBQ shapes?" What are they? I thought.

"We need cheese slices for school lunches."

"And avocado."

"And snacks for play lunch."

It was becoming a long list of forgotten items.

"What's for dinner tonight?"

I wasn't sure. I had bought stuff, rather than ingredients to make up a meal.

There were a few other issues. It turned out that I had lots of cleaning products already; the bin liners were too small for the bin; I had bought so much fresh food that the ham, yoghurts, vegetables and other disposables wouldn't fit in the fridge (maybe I could stir fry them for dinner?); I had added to the already generous supply of 'spag bol' sauce; and I had completely forgotten to buy any chicken.

I realised rather sadly that, despite filling the trolley and spending over $400 on what I thought would be a month's supply of food, I would be going back to Coles again in the next couple of days.

To make matters worse it was lunchtime already. Another morning had passed. I decided to have a more typical Sunday

5 Sunday bloody Sunday

afternoon and focus on the things I knew I could do well, a sort of confidence booster. I mowed the lawn and watched some rugby.

At 9.30 that evening, with the ironing done and the girls in bed, I slumped on the sofa. I momentarily had a feeling of victory, the feeling I used to have at the end of the occasional weekend when my wife had been away and I had looked after the children and the house. I would feel tired, but satisfied that all required tasks had been completed, no one had been injured and the house was neat and tidy. But this time the moment of victory was fleeting. This was not the end—this was just the beginning. I would have to do this all again next weekend, and the next one, and the next one after that. In fact I would need to do this every weekend as well as cook for and look after the girls during the week. I was knackered and just to finish the weekend off nicely it was a workday tomorrow. I needed a day off already.

I had an early night. I already knew that I needed to be much more efficient with my household chores if I was going to have any free time. I started to come up with a few ideas.

I was sleeping in a double bed and, as a creature of habit, was still sleeping on my side. This meant half of the sheet wasn't being used. What if I spent a week sleeping on my side of the bed and then a week sleeping on the other side? That would mean only washing the sheets every two weeks. Mind you it was only me in the bed. What if I slept on each side for two weeks at a time? That would mean I would only need to wash the sheets once a month. Genius! I thought further. What if after the first month I just turned the sheets over and slept on the other side? A whole two months between washes—now we're talking!!

I felt the creative juices start to flow. Using my household equipment meant needing to clean it. I was lucky enough to have a gym at work. What was to stop me from having a shower at work every day rather than at home? My shower at home would then be for weekends only and would probably only need to be cleaned every few months.

Extending the idea of bathrooms—what if I did my 'business' at work rather than at home? That would be a significant saving on the most unpleasant job of them all—toilet cleaning. I needed to think long and hard about this. Doing a No.2 in a public loo was one of my greatest fears—a phobia brought on by a combination of disgust and embarrassment. Firstly, I couldn't bring myself to put my bottom on a seat that some hairy-arsed bloke had recently used (there's nothing worse than the 'just vacated' warmth of a toilet seat). Secondly, I strongly believed that this was a private function and not one to be shared with other men.

I believe my No.2 phobia started when I was at primary school. I remember sitting in class, at ten in the morning, knowing that I had one 'coming through the gates' and wondering whether I had the mental and physical strength to hold on until I got home at something like four in the afternoon. This would have been a significant challenge for a grown man, let alone a six-year-old boy.

By the time the last lesson before lunch came around I was starting to feel quite ill. God knows what damage I was doing to my intestines by keeping this thing, or things, inside me. I decided not to eat at lunchtime for fear of 'topping up' whatever was in progress. But it was to no avail—I broke down during the first lesson after the break. The force of nature was unstoppable and I filled my shorts. The caretaker was called and, in a moment of absolute humiliation, he carried me, chair and all, to the toilet, from where my mum came to take me home. I couldn't go to school the next day as I was so ashamed. Fortunately my mum played along and she concocted some story about a mysterious tummy bug, visits to the doctor, best to be on the safe side and so on.

The phobia has been with me for the rest of my life. I can count on the fingers of one hand the number of occasions when, in cases of extreme emergency, I have been forced to use a public facility. I have horrible memories of a curry house in London; a train station in Bristol; and a Kenya Airways plane. None of these are places I would have chosen to visit had it not been for some hideous bout of food poisoning. Adopting public No.2 delivery as a labour saving device was therefore going to require a massive dose of mental courage.

Some of my other ideas were a little less earth shattering, such as getting a cleaner to help with the housework. I knew this would be quite an expensive option, so the trick was to use the cleaner as part of an overall cleaning plan, rather than simply leaving all of the cleaning to him or her. My approach was simple. I would look after the downstairs, the girls would look after their rooms and the upstairs, and the cleaner would do two hours every two weeks to look after the bathrooms and give the kitchen a good clean. The girls and I would do the easy bits while the cleaner did the harder bits which I hated doing. This way I would get much better value for money. We were a well-drilled and efficient team and I was effectively only outlaying $25 a week on the cleaner. If I avoided the temptation to drink during the week it pretty much paid for itself and got rid of one of my most hated chores. It was a great trade off.

I also took the big decision not to build my future social life around my weekly trip to Coles. My feelings of social excitement and anticipation were becoming more and more subdued as the weeks went by and I failed to spot, let alone make flirtatious contact with, anyone who looked remotely interesting. At the same time, the inane drudgery of parking, wandering the aisles and packing and unpacking the car was becoming more and more frustrating. Plus, on occasions, I was forced to take a longer checkout queue because of the need to avoid Sharni. All in all, it was a couple of hours of my weekend that I wanted back, and I didn't have many spare hours.

I didn't give up on Coles completely because I ventured into the wonderful world of online shopping. This is not just a great labour saving device—you can shop from the comfort of your own office—but it also takes the stress out of weekend shopping. Admittedly, there is quite a lot of work to do to get started, but for a time short single parent it is a fabulous concept. It was quite overwhelming initially—there was so much on the website. There were some fifty-three different types of bread to choose from and another twenty odd types of milk—normal, low fat, no fat, 1L, 2L, 3L etc, etc. And, because I wasn't an experienced shopper, I didn't know what I normally bought and, in particular, how much of something I normally bought.

I found a good way forward was to blend online shopping with regular shopping for a few weeks while I developed a feel for what I needed. I kept my shopping receipts and used them to populate my standard online orders. Generally this worked well, although I still made a few volume errors in the early months. I now know 250g of mixed nuts is not very much and that 2kg of chicken is enough to feed a family of ten. On one occasion, due to an unfortunate slip of the mouse, a whole leg of ham was delivered, instead of the 250g of sliced leg ham I thought that I had ordered.

But with experience I became a proficient user. It's a fantastic way of shopping for basics and getting them delivered to your door—as long as you avoid fruit and vegetables (it's best to see and choose these yourself, otherwise you can end up with a bunch of skanky veg and bruised fruit). As an added bonus my social interactions with the down-to-earth delivery drivers were always much more pleasant, and embarrassment free, than those with Sharni and her associates.

Over time I developed a routine that worked for me. I made sure I always did the washing and went to the butcher and fruit shop on Saturday morning (when they were open!), did my household chores on Sunday morning and ordered a Coles online delivery for a midweek evening. This broadly left both weekend afternoons for free time. It was the only way that I could survive. I had to have order and routine at the weekends otherwise they would get away from me, I would not have enough 'me time' and I would get back to work on Monday feeling terribly frustrated—and I knew that if I stopped performing at work and lost my job then I really would be in trouble.

My routine, with a little bit of refinement, worked well for me over the years and generally ensured I got enough down time. It meant the basics were covered and it gave me time to focus on the really important and difficult challenges—bringing up two teenage daughters.

And anyway the cavalry were arriving; my mum was on her way to Australia.

6

Stiff upper lip

My mum was going to spend some time with me to provide a crash course in running a house, bringing up girls and any other useful skills that might come to mind. But because we English are a strange lot, it nearly didn't happen, and I would have missed out on a very valuable and personally enriching experience.

I imagine that years ago, when one was on the battlefield standing in one's bright shiny uniform—the one that made you stand out as a perfect target—facing a pack of charging Zulus, that the stiff upper lip approach to life was very valuable. Far better to stand to attention, unflinching in the face of danger, and take a spear in the guts, than to suffer the indignity of confiding in the soldier standing next to you that you were, in fact, a little bit apprehensive about the forthcoming hoo-ha, or worse, that you were suffering from a slightly runny botty and would much rather be back at home having a nice cup of tea and a scone. After all, there was no need to be afraid because there was the reassuring comfort of the undisputable fact that God was on your side. What could possibly go wrong? The British Empire was built on the stiff upper lip. Mind you, look at the country now.

So, in the days towards the end of our September holiday in England, before I left to return to Australia and begin my life as a single father, my mother and I, because we are English, adopted the stiff upper lip approach to life. Everyone was asking my shell-shocked mum how she had been coping in the two months since my dad had died and how she was adjusting to life on her own, doing all the things that Dad used to do, keeping it together and learning to start again.

"It's been a bit difficult but I am fine," my mum would reply, smiling brightly. "Don't worry about me. Who's for tea? Shall I put the kettle on?"

And everyone was asking the shell-shocked me the same thing. Would I be all right adjusting to life on my own, doing all the things that my wife used to do, keeping it together and learning to start again?

"It will be a bit difficult but I will be fine," I would reply, smiling brightly. "Don't worry about me. Oh, are you making tea? Lovely."

It was pathetic really. I wasn't fine. I was far from fine. To be honest, I was suffering from a slightly runny botty. The Zulus were beating their drums outside the corral and I had seen what had happened to Michael Caine. He had maintained a beautifully appropriate stiff upper lip but he had also been inconvenienced by a nasty spear wound to the stomach resulting in a brave but incredibly slow and painful death. It was one of the greatest scenes in English film history and Sir Michael wrung every last possible drop of emotion from it.

It turned out that my mum was far from fine as well. I wouldn't go as far as saying that she was suffering from a slightly runny botty, but she had her own fears and she was missing my dad desperately. She was taking things one step at a time but had a long way to go. Apart from the emotional recovery, she had a full list of practical issues to deal with— she hadn't yet worked out how to use the new satellite box for the TV or relight the pilot light for the gas. She was overwhelmed.

We were both putting on a brave face when all we wanted to do was have a good cry and ask for some help. But we are English—so we couldn't. It would be a faux pas equivalent to accidentally brushing your opponent's balls while leaning over the table during a game of snooker. People would mutter and not look you in the eye. It just wasn't done.

It took a flash of South American fire to change the situation and turn it on its head. My brother is married to an Argentine. She doesn't believe in the concept of the stiff upper lip but she does believe in family, and she cut a passionate swathe through our English reserve. She had observed our polite conversation and our unrivalled ability to talk around the issues long enough. And she exploded with passion.

"You two are crazy. Mark, you need help. Your mother doesn't want to be alone. She has no ties to keep her in her house. She can go to Australia at any time and for as long as she wants. Don't you see? She can help you and support you. And it will be good for your mum to have a break and a change of scene and to spend some more time with the girls."

Her words were accompanied by a dramatic toss of her long, dark curls.

God it was awkward. My brother choked slightly on his tea and a little bit escaped from his mouth and ran down his chin. He had to dab it off with his hankie while looking out of the window, pretending to study the local birdlife. I skilfully managed to swallow my tea, even though it was piping hot and scalded my throat, but my eyes remained fixed on my saucer. I couldn't look up. It was too embarrassing. It was right up there with the time a few years earlier when my dad, fresh back from a trip to Argentina and excited to embrace his newly found inner Latin, had held my head in his hands and clumsily tried to kiss me on the lips. I remember our eyes being open and far too close together and the burn of stubble rash. Not nice.

My mum simply had a tear in her eye. When I looked up I said, in that classic English understated way, "Well, I suppose we could think about it."

It was exactly what I wanted and yet I still couldn't bring myself to ask for help. It was what my mum wanted as well, but she hadn't been able to bring herself to suggest it. It was a brilliant idea and I will be forever grateful to my brother's wife for slicing through our ridiculous English reserve and stating what was, after all, the bleeding obvious.

I gave my mum a hug and we agreed that she would come to Australia for a period of some six weeks. She couldn't leave straight away—so I had a head start of ten days. It was a happy and positive goodbye at Heathrow airport, normally when I say goodbye to my mum I don't know when I will see her next.

And so, a couple of weeks later, I was picking my mum up from Melbourne airport. I was pleased to see her, but also sad. I had become accustomed to the sight of Mum and Dad, side-by-side, pushing their trolley together through the arrivals hall. This time it was only Mum. It didn't look right. It re-enforced for me that my dad was gone for good.

It was great having my mum with us. She immediately took over a lot of the domestic duties, which meant I was able to concentrate on the girls' wellbeing and my work. For six weeks we became a new family unit. Three generations living and learning together as we each confronted, and started to deal with, our own demons. My mum was re-living her parenting role from some thirty years ago. I could never have imagined that I would be relying on my mum for day-to-day support at the age of forty-four, and I doubt she ever imagined that she would go back to being a hands-on parent in her late sixties.

But it was as good for her as it was for me. It gave my mum a sense of purpose—she managed the house, did the shopping, did the cooking, did bits of cleaning and drove the girls to dance—and in the evenings we talked about Dad, our lives and what we were going to do next. When I was growing up most of my serious adult conversations had been with my dad and so this was my chance to get closer to my mum and understand something about what made her tick and her hopes and fears for the future.

It was just another example of how, in the middle of the most difficult times of your life, you can still have positive and enriching experiences. I learnt a lot from, and about, my mum—and I became a lot closer to her.

My mum stayed until my birthday in early November. She left a few days later. It was a really difficult day. I returned home from work in the afternoon and found her sitting in the garden reading her book. Our last few hours together were sad. It had been a hugely enjoyable and valuable time but we both knew she couldn't stay forever and that she had to go home. We each had our own lives to lead.

Saying goodbye to my family after a visit to the UK, or after they have been out to Australia, has been by far the most difficult aspect of my living away from them. The build up to the trip is very exciting, the time spent with them is great and then, for the last couple of days, I always get a slightly empty feeling in my stomach in anticipation of the pain of saying goodbye, knowing that I will not see them again for a few years. The goodbye always seems so final.

And saying goodbye to my mum on this occasion was particularly tough. We had been together for six weeks. We hadn't spent this amount of time together since I had left home at the age of twenty-one. During her stay my mum had supported me as a single father and we had supported each other emotionally and grown closer as a result. Now we were going back to lives on our own. It was hard.

We had a quiet reflective drive out to the airport, both of us wondering what the next few weeks would bring and how we would cope. We didn't get too emotional when we said our goodbyes at the airport and I didn't, to my eternal regret, tell my mum how much I loved her. Instead, I went back to stiff upper lip mode and thanked her for helping me out—I made Prince Charles look like a sensitive, new-age guy.

As my mum disappeared through security I shed a little tear. I drove home with an empty passenger seat. The girls were home from school when I got back and we quietly ate the dinner my mum had prepared that morning, a last reminder of the time she had spent with us.

It was a year of massive goodbyes. My dad was gone, my wife was gone, and now my mum was gone and I felt very alone. I knew I would see my mum again. But I also knew that we would probably never again share the closeness of the past six weeks. Thanks again Mum, I love you.

7

Eye of the tiger

Looking back now I recognise that I was lucky. My children were twelve and fourteen at the time of my separation, I had a well-paid job, an understanding employer, who accepted my need for flexibility in my working arrangements so that I could support my family and I was able to keep our family home. If my girls had been much younger at the time I don't know whether it would have been possible for me to hold down my job while they were living with me full-time. I had no family support network in Australia that I could call on to help me, and young children need to spend a lot of time with their mother.

I learnt quickly that the first rule of survival as a single father is to keep it together. I was the pack leader and I needed to look after myself if I was going to look after the girls properly. As a single father, you need to be in good shape both mentally and physically to enable you to deal with your new life, which, until it has settled down, will be full of difficulties and new challenges. It's almost a completely new life, it's a difficult change to adjust to—and it's bloody hard work.

In my case I was still going through the pain of separation, I missed my wife, I had financial stuff to deal with and I had to learn how to run a home and look after the girls. At times there was a massive temptation to take the easy way out and drink my reality away. But the girls were also suffering. They were grieving for the loss of their family and the loss of their mother, and also dealing with their own personal pain and anger. If I was to help them I needed to be strong and set the example. Being a wreck wasn't going to be at all helpful. I needed to be Rocky (the Rocky from the first film, naturally)—except I needed to be able to converse with a slightly broader vocabulary and better syntax, and not jog everywhere in a beanie. I liked this idea and for a few mornings I even played the inspirational *Eye of the Tiger* when I woke up, until I realised I was just being a wanker.

When I first found out about my wife's affair, and knew for certain she would be leaving me, my thoughts were more about her and how I could screw up her plans, rather than about me and what I was going to do. She was very happy and confident about the prospect of her new, improved, and no doubt perfect, life—looking forward to time with her soul mate balanced by time with the children, nice holidays, a new found freedom and so on and so on. Meanwhile I hated the fact that, while she planned her brand new life, I had been left behind and cast off like an old sock. I just wanted revenge. I had a number of ideas:

1. Go back to the UK. This would really rock the boat. It would cramp her new found freedom and turn all her nice, new, lovely plans on their head. She would suddenly be very busy. The kids would miss me and would blame her. It would be a classic 'see you later' moment as I headed off into the sunset with my swag. I would go home, write off my Australian adventure and start all over again with the support of my UK family.

But this wasn't really a good idea—I would be just running away. How could I heap more pain on the girls' shoulders at what was such a traumatic time for them? Hardly the work of a caring father and, anyway, I would miss them too much. Would this be what Rocky would do? Of course not. Time for me to run up and down some more steps.

2. Become George Best. This seemed more promising. I would sell the family home; move into a swanky apartment in the city; live the champagne lifestyle; have a string of ever younger and blonder girlfriends; be the envy of all my friends; and die young with a smile on my face and a gently softening erection in my pants.

On paper a brilliant idea, but with potential flaws. I was forty-four. I was past my prime. I was skinny and newly gaunt with a little gut and asymmetrical testicles. Without the ability to attract blondes (a real risk) I would probably die a sad, lonely old man. Even worse, if the blondes were a little long in the tooth or a bit 'dodgy' then, rather than becoming George Best, I would become an object of ridicule and probably end up dying with a nasty little rash.

3. Become a hermit and adopt the alternative lifestyle. Quit my job; move out of Melbourne; grow my own vegetables; wear a large, baggy brown jumper—all the time; grow my hair; grow a beard; never wash; and sit outside the house all day swearing at people and scaring small children.

I have to confess that this idea had some merit but, ultimately, I do like my creature comforts. Plus, I am a big Manchester City fan—and you need cable TV to watch Premiership soccer.

4. Become a Monk. This was a non-starter. I had already recognised that I didn't want to revert to my old 'tradition' of spending evenings alone, shuffling my pennies.

In truth they were all stupid ideas. Revenge was not a smart strategy and I knew that it would only cause more pain to the people I loved the most—the children. But it's amazing what goes through your head during separation. The only sensible decision was to be strong—for myself and the kids—and to not throw it all away. I resolved that my overall goal would be to give my girls as good a life as I could—and to achieve this I had to be emotionally and physically fit.

It was easier said than done. Going through the break-up was incredibly stressful and the most difficult thing I have ever had to deal with. My main issue in the short term was that I was rapidly becoming a wreck. I made four important resolutions:

1. Get some proper sleep. I was spending most of my nights tossing and turning—fortunately in the traditional sense of the phrase.
2. Get back to the gym. I needed to start to feel good about myself again.
3. Find a friend to talk to. I was keeping too much inside me and I needed to share it.
4. Accept that my marriage was over. Difficult one that.

Firstly sleep. I was finding that I would go to bed knackered, sleep for a few hours, and then wake up at two or three in the morning. Waking up was the cue for me to go through the same thoughts over and over again. How could my wife do this—to me and to the girls? Where had I gone wrong? Why did she want to be with someone else? How could she put her own happiness before that of her children? How could her soul mate make her happy and I couldn't? Should I have seen it coming? What had I done to deserve such a difficult life? And why does England always get knocked out of the soccer World Cup at the quarterfinal stage on penalties? My brain wouldn't let me sleep and, of course, there were no answers to the questions. By the time morning came round I was tired.

Lack of sleep was causing my life to become harder and harder and I was struggling to cope—I had to break the cycle.

The answer turned out to be pretty simple. I went to the doctor and he gave me some pills. At the risk of appearing to be Cliff Richard's life coach, I have to confess that I have never taken recreational drugs of any sort, or pharmaceutical drugs any stronger than Lemsip. I have a, probably irrational, fear that serious drugs will cause me to have an unexpected, untreatable, cataclysmic reaction and, after running around like an eye-bulging madman for a couple of hours, I will simply drop dead.

There has only ever been one exception to this. At the age of forty I had the joy of experiencing circumcision. It was not that I had discovered the Jewish faith and, as a consequence, wanted to put my lady tickler into the care of an ageing and shaky handed Rabbi so that I was 'properly dressed' as it were. No, it was simply that I had a bit of an issue with the flexibility of my foreskin and, sadly, it and I needed to be separated. It was a traumatic moment. This tiny piece of skin had been with me forever and together we had shared some of the best moments of my life, sometimes just the two of us, and sometimes involving others. But now our journey was to come to a close—my future would be one of open top motoring.

My surgeon was a thin, balding chap who had a nice comforting manner. One sunny afternoon, I dropped my trousers and lay on his table while he peered at my equipment and gave it a little poke with a blunt, metal instrument. I noticed that he had reassuringly steady hands, which I felt would be quite important later on. He confirmed that circumcision was the answer to my problem and, in an instant, I was booked in to make my debut on the operating table.

The surgeon and I said our goodbyes with a nice warm

handshake. Again, I felt this would be important later on, I knew I would be unconscious but I thought my little gentleman's sausage deserved better than to experience the shock of a cold touch. As I headed towards the door he looked up.

"How often do you feel your testicles?" he asked me.

"Er, I'm not sure," I replied. I didn't know what the context was and I didn't want to say something stupid. What was an appropriate frequency? Not often enough and he might think that I didn't care about my testes; too often and he might think that I was a mad, bollock-fondler.

"You know, to check for lumps, to check for cancer," he continued.

"Oh. Not very often."

"Would you like me to check now?" he offered.

I heard myself agreeing to this 'check' even though I wanted to say no. I started to undo my trousers for the second time.

"Don't worry about that," he said and, quick as a flash, he manoeuvred his office chair around from behind his desk until he was sitting right in front of me. He unzipped my fly and started to reach in with his fingers.

"Have you got enough room?" I asked, in a slightly unnatural voice.

"Of course. I do keyhole surgery. I'm good at working in confined spaces." A pause. "Have you always had asymmetrical testicles?"

It was bizarre. I stared out of the window at the Melbourne skyline trying to ignore the fact that, just below my eye line, was the balding head of a man, sitting on a chair, gently exploring my testicles. I daren't look down. It was not a totally unpleasant experience, if I'm honest, and I was terrified I would show my appreciation of his art in the traditional manner. *"Margaret Thatcher naked. Margaret Thatcher naked. Margaret Thatcher naked,*" I whispered to my inner-self. It did the trick. It always does.

Investigation complete, he deemed himself happy with the smoothness and health of my testes and said that he was looking forward to seeing me again in a month.

And a month later, I duly came round from the operation to find myself in a hospital room, which I was sharing with an old man. A young nurse was by my bedside.

"How are you feeling?" she asked.

"A bit groggy. Not too bad," I replied.

"Have you had a look?" she inclined her head in the general direction of my midriff.

"Not yet."

"Would you like me to?"

I hesitated. "It's okay. I'd rather do it myself, but thanks for the offer."

She stood by the bedside eyebrows slightly raised. I waited. She waited. I looked at her. She looked at me.

"Can I have a moment?" I asked.

"Sure."

And with that, she turned on her heels and was gone.

With some trepidation I unwrapped the bandages and gingerly explored my new look—I had gone from short and thin to short and swollen. And black. It looked hideous.

The nurse was back.

"How does it look?" Those eyebrows were half raised again.

"A bit swollen and..."

But, before I could find the words to complete the description, I was interrupted by the arrival of the testicle-cupping surgeon himself, all breezy smile and energy.

"Well, how does it look?" he asked.

But again, before I could answer, he was busily getting

into the bandages. All I could see was the top of his balding head—again.

"Oh yes, this is really good," he exclaimed, without looking up. "Nurse, have a look at this, and tell me what you think!"

A half-smile from the nurse and the eyebrows went to full extension as she slowly moved forward. I now had two people bent over my bruised and battered penis. They reminded me of two pigs foraging for truffles in my undergrowth.

"I suppose it won't stay this size?" I heard the nurse ask.

"Oh no," the surgeon replied. "It just looks that thick because of the swelling. It will go down to its normal size over the next couple of days."

"Never mind," murmured the nurse, looking up at me with another half smile and those raised eyebrows.

"Yes. And, if you look closely, you can see he's got asymmetrical testicles!" the surgeon exclaimed.

I looked across at the old man in the bed next to me. He was also smiling, his own eyebrows raised. Bastard. I hope you have something really nasty, I thought to myself.

A few hours later another nurse came round to talk about pain relief and to offer me some industrial strength painkillers to take home.

"Um, don't worry," I said. "I will just take a Lemsip when I get home. Everything will be fine."

She was obviously not used to people turning down her pills. She explained to me, slightly sarcastically I thought, that the reason I was lying comfortably during this conversation was because the general anaesthetic was still in my system. Once this wore off, she continued, the pain from my newly exposed stump would be excruciating, and I would probably end up running around like an eye-bulging madman while trying to keep the end of my willy from touching my underwear or from bouncing off my knees (okay, I have made that last bit up, she actually said from bouncing off my testicles). I took the drugs home with me.

So here I was, several years later, sitting on the side of my bed with a small container of sleeping pills. According to the prescription I was able to take 1—2 pills a couple of nights a week. I decided to take only one the first night, just to be on the safe side. The prescription also stated that I should take the pill thirty minutes before bed, but I was paranoid it might affect me very quickly and that the girls would find me in the morning slumped over the toilet bowl, so I didn't take it until I was safely tucked up in bed. It was marvellous. I slept well and I woke up feeling much healthier after my first good night's sleep for months. Over the next few weeks the pills helped me to establish a good sleeping pattern and, as a result, I was much better placed to deal with whatever was coming my way.

Now, I am not suggesting sleeping pills should be used as a regular part of your life, but if you're not sleeping well you can't deal with the stress that separation brings and you feel like crap. At this point of the process I needed to be strong and able to think clearly about what I wanted and what I needed to do to get it. If your mind is not letting you sleep, go and see your doctor. Tell him, or her, what you are going through and ask for something to help you get some rest. Doctors see plenty of people going through break-ups and mine was both sympathetic and helpful. Be a real man and go see the doc! They are the single father's friend and have plenty of information on other nasty side effects of separation, such as anxiety and depression.

Secondly exercise. It was becoming a bit too easy to spend my evenings sitting on the sofa, watching TV, feeling sorry for myself, ploughing through a mountain of crisps and enjoying just a bit too much of my favourite drink. I once managed to eat a whole tub of ice cream and sink a bottle of red wine while watching *Deep Purple—Live at the California Jam*. And why not? I was sad and lonely, I said to myself by way of justification. But I knew it wouldn't do me any good in the long term, it was great to escape from my reality for a while, but my reality wasn't going to go away.

When it comes to exercise I'm not a gym junkie but I do like to get to the gym a couple of times a week. I don't have aspirations of becoming Charles Atlas (or even Rocky), I just want to be a little less thin and delay the onset of old age. There are plenty of books that talk about the benefits of regular exercise and a good diet, so I don't need to go on about that here. Suffice to say it's all true, but it was even more important for me at this point in my life.

One of the initial issues I had to deal with when my wife left me was a loss of self-esteem. It was hard to get up in the morning feeling positive about myself when my first waking thoughts were that my wife was (a) thinking about the man whom she would rather be with, or (b) was actually with the man she would rather be with. It was not good for the self-confidence and this was a time when I needed buckets of it. Exercise made me feel better about myself and just the fact that I was back in the gym, regardless of how I looked, made me feel more positive about life.

The other reason for keeping in shape is that, although I hadn't given it too much thought at the time, all single men eventually start dating again and, all being well, this will require taking one's kit off. I will deal with this in a later chapter but, suffice to say, I found getting naked in front of someone new to be quite a daunting proposition and I was glad that, when the time came, I was in reasonable shape (and that the room was quite dark).

Thirdly, find a friend. I was keeping far too much of my pain inside and it was eating away at me. To get through this I needed someone to talk to, someone who was prepared to listen to me moan on about how hard life was, how badly I'd been treated, why it wasn't fair and, in my unique case, that I had recently lost my foreskin. Men have a huge genetic disadvantage in this respect compared to women because we are not used to opening up to our mates.

Most of my man-to-man conversations to date had been about the pros and cons of the rolling maul (rugby union for those of you uninitiated in the game they play in Heaven), assembling IKEA furniture (a favourite hobby of mine—no wonder my bloody wife left me), whether big boobs were more important than good legs and which of the original Charlie's Angels was most likely to be a goer. I don't think that at this point in my life I had ever spoken to another man about inner pain and feelings of despair—although I did once have to tell my doctor about the inner pain and feelings of despair associated with a haemorrhoid problem, which was extremely humiliating, particularly when he asked me if I wanted him to take a look. Women are much better at sharing problems and providing each other with strength and support.

My other disadvantage was that my wife had had a long time to think about leaving me and she was getting plenty of emotional support from her soul mate. The first mover advantage was a big one. She had decided a long time before that our marriage had no future and had already grieved for its loss. She had largely dealt with her sadness and pain. Once she had met somebody new and taken the big decision to move on, her main feelings were positive. She was excited about the promise of her new life. She was ready for the future and was much stronger than me mentally. I was on my lonesome, in shock and still coming to terms with what had happened. I wasn't ready for the future. To make it worse, my family and natural support network were on the other side of the world.

My first efforts to find a friend to confide in were not entirely successful. One afternoon at work, when I was looking particularly thin and gaunt, my secretary (or Executive Assistant to give her the correct title) asked me if I was feeling all right. Perfect opportunity. I explained, with my serious face on, that my wife was having an affair, had decided to leave me and that, as a result, I was a little down in the dumps. She looked at me intently for a few seconds and then burst out laughing. For a horrible moment, I thought she was going to start bouncing around the office and break into some hideous routine that involved giving me the finger while chanting 'loser'. She must really hate me, I concluded. But no, she had simply assumed that I was joking. She left me with no choice but to break the cardinal rule of any executive, and I suffered a major outbreak of lip and chin wobble. It wasn't my proudest moment in the office but at least my Executive Assistant now believed me.

Having told one person it was easier to tell more. The responses I got from my male colleagues were interesting, ranging from massive understatement—"that's no good"—to pointing out the potential for a new and liberated sex life—"two weeks after my wife left me I was in bed with two women"—I was impressed—"you can shag all those birds you have been dreaming about"—unfortunately no one had Jennifer Hawkins's number—"go for the ugly ones, they try much harder in bed because they don't know when they'll get another chance"—an interesting alternative strategy.

It's funny how a lot of men jump to a highly unrealistic upside of being single and see it as an opportunity to move into a world of freelance shagging. I had already discounted the George Best option—I just wanted to be a good dad.

The answer, when I found it, was obvious—confide in a woman. I was lucky enough to have a longstanding female work colleague who I had known for a number of years, but, because I'm a bloke, I had never shared any personal stuff with her. I told her over a coffee. When she replied that it was one of the saddest things she had ever heard, I knew she would agree to me unburdening with her from time to time.

Looking back, I now recognise that there were some friends who were able to support me by listening to my tales of woe, some who would give me good advice and practical suggestions and others whose job was simply to make me smile on a dark day. The trick was to find a small number of people who could provide the full range of support that I needed. Not everyone wants to hear your tale of woe, and all some people want to do is daydream with you about shagging opportunities. You just need to work out who is who.

Fourthly, acceptance. It took me a while to accept my marriage was over and for several months part of me believed that I would get home one day to find my wife sitting on the sofa, crying and ready to tell me what a terrible mistake it had all been. This was a little naive given we were just starting our hideous battle of financial settlement. If I had found my wife at home, the chances are that she would have been hiding in the hallway ready to rearrange my face. Despite this reality it was hard to let her go and I often dreamt about her so intensely that sometimes, when I woke up, I was surprised to be alone.

But I did finally get to the point of accepting that she was gone and wasn't coming back. And even if she had come back could our marriage have ever been the same? Would I have been able to trust her? Would her soul mate have still been in her life, lurking in the background? Would I have wanted revenge? Would I have looked for an affair of my own to teach her a lesson? Would I have been able to respect her? Would she have respected me?

In reality we would probably have been stuck in a tense, difficult and unhappy relationship, keeping it together for the sake of the children—would that have been a better life for all of us? Is it better for children if their parents are happy, but not together, rather than unhappy but together?

Despite my growing acceptance, drawing a line under my marriage was hard, partly because I had to recognise, albeit grudgingly, that I had presumably played some role in my wife being 'not happy enough' and wanting to move on, and partly because it meant that my comfortable, familiar life was over forever.

However, in time, I found that with acceptance came determination and strength. This was my reality. I was a new Mark Tucker, I had a new life ahead of me and there was no going back. It was no good mourning the past; I had to live in the present. It had taken a few months but I was feeling stronger. I had a more positive outlook, I was generally sleeping well, the exercise was helping me to feel better about myself and I was starting to build a small support network.

Time to take a deep breath and get on with the job of being a single father. Cue *Eye of the Tiger*—actually, don't.

8

Band of gold

"*For better for worse.*"
"*For richer for poorer.*"
"*Until death do us part.*"

The familiar words that thousands of 'happy couples' recite at their wedding ceremonies.

My wife and I had gone through the ritual willingly. I can't remember whether I thought a lot about those words at the time, or whether I simply recited them as a necessary step in the process of getting married—but that was okay—we had definitely wanted to get married.

I know a lot of people feel that the spirit of the wedding ceremony is more important than the words, particularly words that are hundreds of years old. But I take my hat off to the person who put those vows together because they were really ringing true for me now. Life was getting a lot worse, I was certainly going to be poorer and, one way or another, my wife was going to be in my life until death parted us. The foresight from the 15th century was astonishing. They had managed to create wedding vows that are still relevant for 21st century life—regardless of whether the marriage survives or not.

In the early months after my wife left me our relationship went from something that had been strong and loving for most of its seventeen years to an absolute nightmare. It was amazing how quickly what I thought had been a positive relationship turned to one driven by anger and, strong though it seems, hate. My wife didn't want this to happen, she wanted to keep our relationship positive. She spoke about the need to keep things amicable, to be reasonable and to avoid a train wreck. It was easy for her—she was the one who had done the leaving, so of course she wanted things to remain positive. And if things stayed amicable she would be able to feel less guilty about what she had done. But it was far from easy for me; I was the one who was hurting. I was angry, feeling stupid, dealing with all of the 'how can she do this to me and the girls?' stuff. I didn't want a train wreck either, but I was a long way from feeling amicable.

And anyway, how was this ever going to be an amicable split? We hadn't talked it over as a couple and come to the joint conclusion, with sadness and regret, that we couldn't keep things together. She wanted to move on—and quickly. She still "cared for me" and "wanted me to be alright", but was that for my benefit or hers? From her perspective it would be a lot easier to tell her family and friends that, despite the fact she had been having an affair, that our marriage was over and that she was now living with her soul mate, I was understanding/happy/supportive of her (delete as applicable) and was getting along just fine. Highly unlikely. About as likely as Ricky Ponting walking after nicking one to the 'keeper. It would have taken the patience of Saint Francis of Assisi for me to feel good about what had happened and to have positive thoughts towards my wife—and I was rapidly turning into Saint Francis of Fuck You Up.

I don't know whether I was always going to be a complete prick about our marriage break-up, but I think my mind was made up in only the second week post separation. It was back in the September holidays when I was in the UK with my children, taking a break from the pain of getting to the day of actual separation and spending time with my family grieving for my dad. With all the subtlety of a Serena William's overhead, my wife thought this would be an appropriate time to send me a rather pithy letter from her lawyer explaining how, in black and white, and sprinkled with generous helpings of legal mumbo-jumbo, our life would be pulled apart.

It was a long document setting out her view of the childcare arrangements, the timing for selling the house, how our finances would be split, the future costs that I would be responsible for, how much child support I would be paying her and so on and so on. Amicable? I wasn't sure how a set of demands from her lawyer fell into the 'amicable separation' category. Train wreck? She was driving the train through the buffers and out through the back of the station.

It was a nightmare—how could this be happening? Less than six months ago I had thought that we were happily married, and now a lawyer had decided how the life that my wife and I had carefully built together for ourselves and our children was going to be disassembled—and disassembled in a matter of months. It was so cold, ruthless and quick. Seeing the names and dates of birth of my children in a lawyer's letter seemed to de-personalise them and reduce them to 'chattels'—the legal term for the things that you have grown to love but are actually, in fact, disposable. My house, our family home, bluntly referred to as "the former matrimonial residence".

It was long and hideous and way too early for me to think about. I realised that I had two options. I could either rollover and give in to her demands, thus ensuring that by doing what was best for her we had an amicable relationship and I avoided stress—at the expense of what was best for me or what I wanted, of course. Or I could fight. I sent back a rather rude and unhelpful email and the battle lines were drawn.

It was on. My wife became Brett Lee again, all pace, venom and snorting fire. For the first few overs all I could do was hang in, duck bouncers, take the hits to the body and try and survive. She was well prepared, again the benefits of first mover advantage and of having time to think it through—she had even been to see her lawyer before we had formally separated and her 'pre-season' training was paying off. I suffered a barrage of requests, legal letters and demands. But eventually, as happens to all fast bowlers, she started to tire, the ball softened, the pitch slowed down, I began to get my eye in—and I became Geoff Boycott, the stubborn Yorkshire cricketing icon. Mine was a simple game plan. I needed time and she needed my wicket, so I took no risks and played a straight bat to every delivery, dot ball after dot ball. I frustrated the crap out of her.

For two people who were once well aligned, my wife and I had some very bizarre interactions as we negotiated the rocky road of learning to be separated. In the first week back from our September holiday to England she came round to the house to see the girls and to talk financial settlements. She had the letter from her lawyer that she had sent to me while I was away and wanted to go through some of the 'points' that I didn't like. I disengaged while she patiently tried to explain why what she was suggesting was fair. I didn't care about the 'points'; I just wanted her to go away. Halfway through her diatribe she looked up.

"That's a nice T-shirt," she remarked.

I just grunted.

"Did you get it while you were away?"

I grunted again. The girls had chosen it for me. It was a good T-shirt and I liked it.

"The colour suits you", she continued—and then went back to the 'points'.

Was this an example of a woman's legendary multi-tasking capability? Or was it because, despite all the crap that she had inflicted on me, she still cared a bit? I didn't get it. I found it hard to understand how these moments of normal conversation could punctuate our bitter arguments.

The other thing I found hard to understand was that she was still wearing her wedding ring. I had thrown mine away, which had seemed nicely symbolic at the time, although I subsequently wondered whether a trip to Cash Converters might have been more practical. I could have taken the $50 they probably would have offered me and bought a nice memento of our failed marriage, a chrome toilet brush for example, so that every time I cleaned the toilet I would be reminded that my marriage had gone down the shitter. Failing that, I could have spent it on a stripper.

"Why are you still wearing your engagement and wedding rings?" I asked her.

She thought about it for a second.

"Well, we *are* still married," she replied.

I couldn't fault the logic.

"Don't you think it's strange that you are living with one man and wearing another man's ring? Don't you think the wedding ring represents a life we had that is now over?"

"It's a nice piece and I hadn't really thought about it," she concluded.

I wasn't happy. To me the ring was a symbol of our, admittedly failed, marriage and not simply a "nice piece".

"I want the rings back," I demanded, sounding a bit like a

spoilt toddler. "I gave them to you and I don't think you have the right to still wear them."

"You gave them to me and you can't take back gifts," she replied.

This was starting to sound like an argument between a pair of four-year-olds. I wondered whether we were going to start trying to push each other over.

"Do you wear them when you are in bed with him?" Churlish, I know, but I was frustrated and hurt and wanted to get personal.

As with many of our post-separation arguments we both had completely different positions, both thought that we were right and quickly became angry with each other. But, short of ripping the rings off of her finger, there was not much I could actually do to get them back.

Amazingly, the next time I met her the rings were gone. Maybe she had gone home to the soul mate, raised the concept that it might be inappropriate to wear another man's rings and they had realised that I was right. Victory! When would I be getting them back? In my mind I was already in the car to Cash Converters.

But alas, no victory. When I pointed out, rather smugly, that I had been right about the rings she explained that she was now going to wear them on the fourth finger of her right hand instead—they were such nice pieces after all—and that they needed to be re-sized to fit. To make matters worse she had also decided to hand them down to the girls in due course. Great. I half expected to be sent the bill for the re-sizing.

9

Absolute beginners

Of all the things I have achieved in my life, growing into my role as a single father and bringing up two wonderful girls is the one that I am most proud of. I know every parent dotes over their kids and thinks that they are brilliant. But when you are the main provider, guide and shoulder to cry on, being with them as they clear life's milestones and challenges is a much more intense parenting experience. My children were going through the normal growing up stuff and I was going through it with them—making and falling out with friends; starting highschool; going to parties; getting drunk; meeting and splitting up with their first boyfriend and so on.

The upside of my divorce is that I have been a far more important part of the girls' lives than I would have been if my marriage had survived. I simply wouldn't have needed to have had such a strong focus on them and their day to day lives because that would have been my wife's focus. I would have been busy earning the money to pay *for* their lives, without necessarily making a significant contribution *to* their lives. I would have happily played the 'traditional' role of the father, i.e. the provider, and missed out on the real experience of their growing up. And the sad thing is, I wouldn't even have realised that I was missing out.

My life with the children has been much richer, the good

times more rewarding and the hard times tougher. Caring for my children and helping them to grow up became the central theme of my life. In fact, it defined my life. It was a massive, fundamental change in outlook, and at the heart of this change was sacrifice. Obviously, there was the financial sacrifice that every parent is aware of but now there was also the sacrifice of time. Time devoted to the children formed the basis of our growing bonds. I strongly believe that time is the greatest gift a parent can give to their children. Probably the ultimate sacrifice. Doing things for, and with, my children caused our love for each other to deepen. In hindsight, it has been a fantastic chapter in my life and, despite the difficulties, I have learnt from it and grown enormously.

In the early months I was very firmly in the 'absolute beginner' category of parenting. I was a learner, living life one day at a time, and my main objectives were practical and focussed on getting the household management under control. I didn't spend much time on building my parenting skills and, as a consequence, I was a reactive, rather than a proactive, parent. I was in catch-up mode. The girls would do something and I would act in response and learn from it. I was more a follower than a leader. This shouldn't have been a surprise to me—after all they had a lot more experience of being kids than I had experience of being a proper parent. But I knew that if I was to make a good job of parenting then I needed to eventually become more proactive, to anticipate what was happening and to be one step ahead of the girls. I also knew this would take both time and effort.

As I've previously said, my goal was to give my daughters the best childhood I could, or at least as 'normal' a childhood as I could, and this meant a significant change in focus. I now had two major elements to my life—raising two children and going to work. Every working man and woman I know talks about 'work/life balance'—how important it is and how difficult it is to achieve. I had been trying to develop a better work life balance for years and now, more by accident than design, I had taken a massive step forward in achieving it.

During the first six months of my separation my youngest daughter was still at primary school, and so I had no choice but to get to work at 9.30am each morning after dropping her off at school. Similarly, I had no choice but to leave work at 5.45pm to make sure I was home in time to make dinner. Fortunately, my company was very supportive of my new working model and I was lucky in this regard—I don't believe many organisations would have been as understanding as mine.

It meant a rebalancing of my priorities—and I loved it. My working day was shortened and so I had to become much more efficient with my time in the office. I made sure that I concentrated on what absolutely had to be done, rather than what might need to be done. I was definitely not 'sweating the small stuff'. It's amazing how much 'stuff' you deal with at work that just gets in the way of doing the things that really matter and then getting home to your family. I became a 'no stuff' person and worked more effectively as a result. I gave up the morning coffee/bitching sessions, I delegated more and got rid of any time consuming parts of my job that actually didn't matter to anyone. I was focussed. I planned each day carefully to get through the important things that needed to be finished before I left the office and got back to the children, and I prepared a 'homework' pile of things that I could do later in the evening if I needed to.

But the most significant change was that work no longer defined me and, as a result, I worried about it less—after all, I had more important things to worry about. And with less worry and stress I became more effective and got more done. The virtuous circle that management books preach and now, because I had no choice, I had become successful at it. So successful, in fact, that a year after my separation I was promoted.

That's not to say there was no stress associated with raising two teenage girls. Far from it—sometimes life with the girls could make office politics look like *Playschool*.

One of the things I enjoyed most about this time was being closely involved in my daughters' developing social lives. We were lucky enough to have a pool in the back garden. I have always seen this as a real luxury and I have enjoyed the challenge of using my schoolboy chemistry skills to keep the acid balanced and the salt and chlorine levels topped up. Kids love pools and over the years it has been a magnet for the girls and their friends through each phase of their growing up. When they were younger the pool was all about swimming and having fun; and as they grew older the hanging out and sunbaking aspects of pool life became more important than the getting wet aspects.

Over time I became used to having lots of girls coming to visit. I was happy for my daughters to bring their friends home, as the alternative was me not knowing where they were, or what they were doing. I loved experiencing their growing up and, probably because I was a relatively chilled parent, their friends enjoyed being at our house. Although this wasn't always without its challenges.

I'm an Englishman so, as you might expect, I am quite partial to a bit of sunbaking and a few lengths of breaststroke (the only stroke that allows you to swim without getting your hair wet—I swim like my mother). However, given the vagaries of the Melbourne weather, i.e. that it may only be hot for one weekend a month, there was sometimes a peak time clash at the pool. There were occasions when I would get home from walking the dogs on a hot day, looking forward to a cooling swim, only to find a bunch of young girls either in the pool or lazing around the side. There were other times when I would be in the pool, or doing something in the garden, when one of my daughters and a group of her friends would turn up, all trendily turned out in their funky bikinis.

One of my rules was that I wouldn't go anywhere near the pool when the girls and their friends were sunbaking or swimming. I was happy to swim with my daughters, but not with their friends now they were becoming young ladies. It just didn't feel right. My girls didn't really get this.

"What are you doing today?" I would ask, on a hot Sunday morning.

"I'm having a few girls over for a swim," would be a typical reply from one of the girls.

"Okay. I will have a quick dip before they get here."

"You don't need to keep out of the way Dad. You can go swimming with us if you like. We don't mind, and all the girls like you."

It was kind of her to offer to share the pool but she didn't appreciate my fear. I could imagine a very awkward conversation between one of Sophie's friends and their father. Something along the following lines:

Friend's dad: "What did you do today?"

Friend: "I went to Sophie's house for a swim."

Friend's dad: "Is she the girl who lives with her father?"

Friend: "Yes."

Friend's dad: "The father who lives there on his own, without a wife?"

Friend: "Yes. He's really nice and friendly and he got in the pool and mucked around with us."

Friend's dad: "Did he just." As he starts to tense up, puts the newspaper down and calls out to his wife.

I knew what the friend's father would be thinking, and I would be thinking the same thing if the roles were reversed. Swimming with other people's daughters is not a good thing to do. I remembered the John Wayne Westerns of my youth, where the local drunk was driven out of town by a posse of angry men while being pelted by eggs and spat upon by the womenfolk. I didn't want that to happen to me.

Despite my fears, the popularity of the house continued to rise and soon a major moment in my life with the girls arrived— hosting their dance school's summer break-up party. Dance was a huge part of both my daughters' lives. They would spend several hours a week at the dance studio learning ballet, jazz, funk, contemporary and all sorts of dance styles. They loved it. They had a great bunch of friends there and they were very supportive of each other. It was a real family environment. The end of year break-up party was therefore a massive event. It was an honour to host it—and it had to go well. The girls and I planned it together over several weekends.

We sorted out the drinks, the snacks, the music and the decorations. This was something I had never done with them before. It was fantastic to see how their minds worked and how passionate they were about the party. These were the times when we bonded and grew as a family unit—getting involved in things that were important to the girls, dedicating real time to them and taking their interests seriously. Serious involvement from me that showed love and care was reflected in a similar response from the girls and helped to build the foundations of our relationship.

Eventually the planning was over and the day of the party arrived. One Saturday afternoon some thirty girls aged from twelve to eighteen came round to the house to sit in the sun and look back on the year—the hard work of rehearsals, the trauma of injuries, the embarrassment of being perved at by old men during shopping centre performances and the success of the big, end of year concert. All the girls seemed to have taken the life of a dancer to the extreme and the garden was full of pirouettes, stretches and moves being busted. The party was a great success. The girls were perfect hosts and we worked well as a team.

As I surveyed the happy scene, I was surprised to see a lone boy amongst the guests, who seemed to be spending most of his time happily massaging the scantily dressed girls. I didn't want to appear to be a fussy father but I thought some parental intervention might be required. I made up a jug of orange squash and went out into the garden on the pretence of serving it. I had a discrete word with my eldest daughter.

"I'm a bit worried about that boy over there, he seems too familiar with the girls," I said, trying to be sensible about it.

"Don't worry," Sophie replied. "That's Dylan and he's gay, no one cares."

As I walked back into the house, Dylan briefly interrupted his delivery of pleasure to one of the older girls, glanced up at me and smiled. Great bluff I thought—but they will hate you when they discover the truth.

10

Let's talk about sex

One of my first formal parental duties was to take my youngest daughter to 'Sex Education' at her primary school. Everybody knows that failed marriages are a major source of interest, speculation, gossip and entertainment across the community, as people attempt to separate fact from fiction. Break-ups are similar to major accidents and, despite the trauma and sadness of the situation, there is a morbid fascination to find out the details. Who pulled the pin? Is it amicable? Is the house on the market? Is there somebody else involved? How are the kids dealing with it? And then there are the rumours: "They haven't slept together for months", "She caught him with the cleaner", "He always leaves the toilet seat up", "She spent all their money on commercial quality kitchen blenders", "He watches porn all night"—and so on.

With this backdrop I was about to enter the hornet's nest of speculation—the Year 6 parents concentrated as a single, amorphous mass in the school hall. This was going to be a real challenge for me. It was my first public appearance as a single father and I knew that this group of parents would be waiting for me with eager anticipation. What will he look like? Is he coping? Does he appear to be struggling?

People also tend to be polarised about who is to blame for a marriage break down and have a tendency to support one of the split parents more than the other. There are no fixed rules and at times no logic about who gets the support and so, as I walked into the school hall, I had no way of knowing which of the assembled parents thought I was the bad guy and who thought I was the victim. I didn't even know if some people were wondering whether I was a porn addict.

There was some shuffling in seats, a few nudges and, I thought, a sense of hush (which I may have imagined) as I went into the hall.

I decided to walk in confidently—a man in control—and I met the odd glance that came my way with a smile. And I did feel confident. I was coping and my daughter was smiling. She was well turned out, her socks were matching and she was excited to see her friends in an after school environment. And besides, what could they tell a twelve-year-old girl about sex that I didn't already know?

I started to feel a little less comfortable as I looked around and realised that the hall had been divided into two halves—boys with their fathers, and girls with their mothers.

"The form said I should sit with the fathers," I bluffed my daughter.

"Okay, I'll sit with my friends then," she replied.

That wasn't quite the reaction I was hoping for. I could either continue the bluff and run the risk that we might end up sitting on separate sides of the hall, or I could sit with her on the female side. One thing was certain—she wasn't going to sit amongst a group of boys while they, no doubt, talked about condoms, 'banging some chicks' and how Sex Ed was really lame because they knew it all and had already done it all. I couldn't really blame her for that. I weighed it up. I would rather sit with the boys and their dads but this would largely defeat the purpose of me attending and, as I looked at them, I recognised that it was a tight knit group—one dad, one son. If I sat with them it was highly likely one of the more astute fathers, or worse one of the kids, would realise that I was joining in a discussion on what little boys get up to when they are alone, without a little boy of my own to justify my participation. I could imagine people starting to whisper and shift uncomfortably in their seats, wondering who the interloper was, the hubbub building into a groundswell of concern and then a particularly large bloke with Dickensian sideburns, a waistcoat and top hat (I don't know why—it's just what I imagined) standing up, pointing at me and, in a loud booming voice, uttering the words, "Gentlemen, we have a pervert in our midst". This would then be the cue for a full-on riot breaking out.

On balance sitting with the women and the girls felt like a better option.

"Do you mind if my *daughter* and I sit here," I said, in far too loud a voice. I didn't want there to be any doubting the legitimacy of my attending the education session, or my right to be part of the female section. I sat there rather sheepishly, a lone male in a sea of some fifty girls and their mothers, while the Sex Ed team ran through a series of pictures of sexual organs, drawings of fallopian tubes and a rather gruesome description of the monthly cycle, all leading up to the climax (if I may use that expression in the context of Sex Ed) in which a little old lady recounted the tale of a sperm called Steven, who went on a journey of discovery and won the race against his other friends from the semen shed (okay, she didn't actually use that last term). I spent a lot of time examining the ceiling and occasionally 'checking in' with my daughter, as the pre-event literature suggested, to make sure that she was coping with these shocking revelations and to deal with any concerns she might have.

"Does it all make sense?" I whispered, hoping there wouldn't be any awkward questions.

"It's a bit boring," she replied. "The *Knocked Up* version is way funnier." Great, I thought.

The next item on the agenda was a Wiggles-style song about the sperm and the egg, which I think even the kids found a bit lame, and this was followed by a most bizarre session in which the little old lady asked the girls and boys to call out alternative names for their sexual organs, which she duly wrote up on a flipchart. I don't know if I was the only parent who found it slightly disturbing to hear a little, grey-haired, old lady say things like "Yes Michael, 'cock' is a correct term for 'penis'." Her elocution was perfect and she over-exaggerated the vowels—which I think was the most disturbing thing of all.

Out came the terms, each one repeated by the little old lady and faithfully reproduced on the flipchart.

From the boys: 'willy'; 'knob'; 'dick'.

From the girls: 'muff'; 'front bottom'; 'fanny'.

I thought the last one a bit risky, but they were all taken with a smile by the little old lady, who kept her cool and remained completely un-phased by it all. I relaxed. This was a bit like a drinking game, I was probably laughing a bit too loudly but it was just a natural way of getting rid of my initial tension.

The kids grew in confidence. 'Middle stump'; 'the probe'; 'the cave that grips'; 'pocket piccolo'. On and on it went, the intensity and excitement level steadily rising to fever pitch, until a boy shouted out "My dad calls his the whore pipe." That brought the session to a premature end (again, if I may use that phrase in the context of Sex Ed), while everyone turned to see which unfortunate father was apparently spending his evenings in hostels of ill repute. We all took a mental note for reference in case his marriage ever broke up.

The final segment brought me right back down to Earth and made the reason for the segregated seating painfully apparent. It was now time for the mothers to talk to their girls about their first period and for the fathers to talk to their boys about their first wet dream. I was horrified. Was this appropriate for twelve-year-olds? Regardless of the answer it presented me with a dilemma. I had never had a period, although I suspected my experience of haemorrhoids was probably fairly similar, and I was definitely not prepared to talk to my daughter about my first wet dream.

For a moment I felt like running to the boys' section but I knew that such a sudden move would be a bad look. I was starting to panic but, fortunately, one of the mothers, who I knew quite well, took pity on me and invited my daughter to join her little group. I thanked her, offered to return the favour at some point (I had no idea what I was saying, my mouth was on autopilot due to shock) and told her that I would wait outside. She had done me a great kindness and I felt it would be improper of me to listen to the story of her first period.

11

Message in a bottle

As I got more used to my new single dad role, I felt that I was beginning to move from the beginner stage of parenting to the intermediate stage. There were no significant moments to mark this milestone; I just seemed to have things more under control and a better understanding of what needed to be done. I was more on the front foot, better able to anticipate what was coming up, more understanding of the girls' needs and more confident in my own abilities.

I had made great strides forward in my household management, my routine was working effectively and so I now had more time for myself. Meals were beginning to improve and a few signature dishes—or at least relatively popular dinners—were beginning to emerge. My work/life balance was going well and I was getting my career back on track. Life was certainly busy but it had become manageable. However, as I was maturing as a parent, the girls were also maturing as teenagers. They were starting to find their way in the world and with this came new and bigger challenges.

I was sure that I was much closer to my daughters than I had been when I was living with my wife. They were adamant they could tell me everything and that comforted me. But I should have checked the small print—a child who says they *can* tell you everything is very different from a child who actually *does* tell you everything. So, although I thought we were close, and we had good conversations about our new life and how they were feeling—and even how I was feeling—there were things that I just did not know about. And it turned out that some of these were quite important.

I knew that my eldest daughter had been hit hardest by the end of my marriage and that she now had a difficult relationship with her mother. But I also assumed because she had a good relationship with me that she was coping with the situation. She seemed happy on the outside, she had a busy life, her schoolwork was good, she was sociable and she loved her dancing. This all seemed to paint a picture of a happy, normal child and I didn't think I had anything serious to worry about.

I now know that young teenagers can harbour dark thoughts and, if they become friends with another teenager in a similar state of mind, their feelings can feed off each other, escalate and become more extreme. I was completely unaware that, in my eldest daughter's mind, life was unfair, the world was against her and she had been dealt a terrible blow. Some of her friends, seeing similar unfairness and issues in their own lives, were encouraging these thoughts and, as a group, they were developing ideas of self-harm and, impossible though it was to believe, some of them were even talking about 'ending it all'.

How could a fourteen-year-old have such dark thoughts? Why would a child consider self-harm, or an even more extreme act? Is it because they don't understand the consequences? Is it because they don't understand the importance of talking to their parents? Don't they understand that these feelings will pass, are linked to growing up and that life will get better?

I don't profess to know a lot about the complex life of a teenager but I was horrified when I found out what was going on in my daughter's head, and doubly horrified that I only found out because another adult told me.

One night my eldest daughter was found, in the early hours of the morning, drinking with a friend on a nature strip. Their impromptu party was discovered by my daughter's dance teacher, of all people, who was on her way home after a night out. I had dropped my daughter off at a different friend's house earlier in the evening assuming this would be just another sleepover. I was stunned that she had managed to find her way to another suburb and was now sitting on a nature strip, drinking, at three in the morning. Clearly there was a lot that I still needed to learn about her specifically, and teenagers in general.

Fortunately, because of the family nature of the dance school, a lot of the girls confided in the dance teacher. I'm still not sure whether it was a coincidence that she happened to be driving past that night, or whether she knew the girls were there (more likely), but I am grateful she found them and was able to tell me a little of what the girls had told her. I didn't get all the details, I wasn't aware the patient/doctor and lawyer/client confidentiality principles extended to dance teacher/student, but I was told enough to recognise that I couldn't take Sophie's happiness for granted and that I needed to be far more aware of what she was doing when I wasn't around.

It was an enormous wake-up call. I realised a number of things—one, that I would never know everything about what my daughters were thinking and doing; two, that a smiley and happy child on the outside is not necessarily a happy child on the inside; and three, that children may prefer to confide in other adults rather than their parents.

Life was going to be a lot more complicated than I had originally thought. And so it proved. A couple of months later there was another incident involving my eldest daughter and alcohol—although this one I am happier to put down to a rite of passage.

At around midnight one Saturday night I was woken by a call from a mobile number which I didn't recognise.

"Hello," I mumbled into the phone.

"Oh hi, it's Anna, I think you need to come and get Sophie." It was one of her friends.

"Is she okay?" I asked, which I immediately realised was a stupid question.

"Kind of, but I think she needs to go home."

Out of bed, clothes on, in the car and off to the party, a pool party no less, where I had dropped Sophie a few hours earlier. When I found her I realised that her friend Anna had a fantastic gift for understatement. I didn't think Sophie was 'kind of okay', I thought she was in a bad way. She was slumped in a chair, wrapped in a towel and seemingly unconscious.

"She might have had a bit too much to drink," her friend chipped in helpfully.

No shit, Sherlock—that much was obvious.

"What has she been drinking?" I asked. Did people spike drinks at private parties?

"Just a bottle of vodka, nothing weird."

Bloody hell, I thought. A bottle of vodka would kill me.

I managed to get Sophie to her feet, still wrapped in the towel, and somehow supported her dead weight as we went outside. She seemed able to walk, even though her head was lolling and her eyes were closed—she was doing a fair impression of a zombie from *Sean of the Dead*. She tried to get into the first car on the driveway (which wasn't mine) and then the next car on the driveway (which wasn't mine either). As we made our unsteady progress away from the house, her friends spurred her on with words of encouragement and advice: "Remember the time I got drunk at Andy's and could hardly walk, I was fine the next day."

"I'll look after your Cruisers."

"I'll make sure Tom doesn't get off with anybody else."

"Don't worry about the towel."

"Don't forget to drink some water." A bit late for that, I thought. Still, it was vaguely comforting that her friends had her best interests at heart.

I managed to get her into the car, put the seat belt on and carefully laid the towel across her lap. She took this as an invitation to throw up, and then immediately returned to zombie mode and went back to sleep. I drove home with Sophie starting to lean on me more and more, until finally she was slumped on my shoulder. Her breath was causing my eyes to water and I was worried that it was so alcohol heavy it was going to make me drunk as well. I had to open the window.

We pulled up in our driveway and the zombie next to me spoke.

"I'll be fine," she slurred, and promptly went back to sleep.

I got her out of the car and held her up as we started to walk to the front door.

"I'll be fine," she slurred again.

So I let her go, and watched her walk in a perfect semicircle across the lawn and back towards the road. Interesting. I grabbed her and with a bit of difficulty got her into the house, up the stairs and into bed, still wearing her bikini. I arranged a number of puke collecting vessels around her bed, went downstairs and tucked myself back into my own bed. I couldn't get back to sleep. What if she did a Bon Scott and drowned in her own vomit? Should I make sure she was sleeping on her side—would that be safer? I was worried so, ten minutes later I went back into her room to check on her. Incredibly, she had managed to get out of her bikini, put on her pyjamas and get back into bed. She was now snuggled up in the duvet. She will be fine, I thought, and so I went back to bed—again.

In the morning there was no sound from her room and so, at around ten o'clock, I went back upstairs to investigate. I wondered what a hungover daughter would look like and how she would be coping with what I assumed, perhaps naively, was her first experience of the after-effects of too much alcohol. I was amazed to see her sitting up in bed already logged onto Facebook, presumably getting an update on what had happened at the party after her early departure.

"How are you?" I asked, with some incredulity.

"I'm fine," she replied, as if nothing had happened. "I'll be down for breakfast soon."

Up and about and ready to eat—I was impressed by her ability to recover.

"Are you going to give me a talking to about the dangers of alcohol?" she asked, very sweetly.

"I think I should, don't you?" Although I hadn't thought through how I was going to tackle this or what I would say.

"Not really. I know my limits. I just spent too long in the spa and the alcohol must have affected me more quickly than normal."

A fifteen-year-old who knew her limits? How the bloody hell had she got to know what her limits were. I wasn't sure I would win a rational argument on the dangers of excessive drinking so I went for a different approach.

"Sophie. Just think about it. You were at a pool party in your bikini. You drank too much. You were sick. When you were bending over the bucket throwing up the boys were probably looking at your bum. To make it worse, your boobs probably fell out of your bikini top."

It was brutal but effective. She didn't care about what her friends thought about her throwing up, but she did care about them getting a close up look at her bum and/or boobs. She looked worried for the first time.

"Maybe you're right, I need to be more careful in future," she said, with a slightly distant look on her face.

She hurriedly went back to Facebook to search for incriminating pictures and to seek confirmation from her friends that her new found fears would not be realised.

Bingo, I thought. I'm getting good at this.

12

Beautiful girls

Six months or so into my life as a single father something strange and mildly disturbing happened to me—I got horny. It was quite a sudden thing. I hadn't had any real interest in engaging with members of the opposite sex on either a platonic or physical basis. I was living as a quasi-monk and I had no real desire for getting it on with anyone other than myself.

But now, as if I were a young man and spring was around the corner, I was beginning to experience a slight stirring in my loins. It was a bit like being a teenager again. I would find myself staring at women in the street and daydreaming during meetings. Not a good way for a man of forty-five to behave. It was time to get a service.

But how, who and where? I hadn't been in the dating market for an awfully long time. How was I supposed to go about finding somebody and where would I go to find them? Of course, I had often fantasised about walking into a perfect, ultra-cool bar and talking to groups of attractive funny girls who would laugh at my witty stories. But my recent memories of trips to bars were that they were a bit on the loud side and, because of my years of Whitesnake and AC/DC concerts, I would struggle to follow the conversation above the background noise. Plus, who would I go with? I only had a few single male friends and they were either a lot older or a lot younger than me. I had plenty of married friends who were suspiciously keen on a night of bar cruising and the entertainment of witnessing my attempts to engage with the opposite sex. I could see it now. The lads in a group, egging me on, pushing me out into the middle of the bar (or worse—the dance floor) and in the direction of a group of girls. It would be a glorious, mid-life crisis style, stag night. I had no doubt that my friends would enjoy it more than me—again, living vicariously through my misfortune.

In my youth it had all been so easy. As a student in the mid-80s, I had once bumped into a girl on the dance floor at a heavy rock disco and happily head-banged and air-guitared away with her for an hour without exchanging a word. She was a classic 80s rock chick—black T-shirt, tight jeans, big hair, elaborate waistcoat. Marvellous. At the end of the night we simply went back to her place and were soon engaged in a few 'dirty deeds done dirt cheap'. There were no mobile phone numbers, hotmail addresses, Facebook pages (or even condoms, for that matter) to deal with. It was simply a case of "See you next week". Does that kind of thing still happen? Apparently it does, so my eldest daughter tells me.

Anyway, no time for a nostalgia trip, back to the present and the key question—what sort of woman should I be looking for? After some serious thinking I devised a number of categories in order to narrow my search:

1. A pole dancer (or similar); probably blonde; ultra hot; ultra sexy; great body; and highly intelligent (i.e. only doing the job for the money before resuming a legal career). Obviously this option had a number of downsides. Firstly, her working hours and my working hours were likely to be completely different, so we wouldn't get to see each

other much. Secondly, while all my friends would be totally jealous, I would be a bit worried that she might be looking for opportunities to make a little extra on the side with them. Although this was her profession, would I be able to allow my friends to get upfront and personal with my girlfriend, not forgetting all of the other punters she would be engaging with on a daily basis? Would I end up being the jealous one?

2. A beautiful woman, who loves children, but doesn't have any of her own and doesn't want any. In my mind this was Cameron Diaz. Spunky, funny, smart, hot (but in a more subtle way than the pole dancer). The kind of girl everyone loves. I couldn't see any downside to this option at all, apart from the nagging thought that any woman who loved children and didn't have any of her own would probably want some of her own—unless of course she had been the victim of some unfortunate sterilising mishap. Clearly it might be hard to find someone in this category, although I wondered whether, if I watched enough episodes of *Oprah*, *The View* and *Ellen*, or ploughed through Google, I might find such a victim.

3. A woman over the age of thirty. This was not actually one of my categories but a constraint imposed by my eldest daughter. She felt very strongly that it would be inappropriate for me to go out with someone who was closer to her age than mine. This was a fair call and a thirty-year-old represented the cut off point. I did, however, recognise that this constraint might actually eliminate the Pole Dancer category in its entirety, leaving me with the unobtainable Cameron Diaz-type.

The other, and probably best, way forward was simply not to be too prescriptive and to take whatever I could find. The 'ugly girls' suggestion from my early days of singlehood came back into my mind. Maybe that was the voice of experience speaking, and maybe I should listen to it.

The next question to resolve was the sort of relationship I wanted with this woman. I didn't want a wife, I already had one of those and things weren't going too well at the moment, so that was clearly off the table. Did I want something casual or a bit more serious? Did I want a significant relationship and run the risk that it might interfere with my relationship with my children? Or did I just want some company for Saturday nights?

It became clear that this wasn't going to be an easy exercise so, to provide a bit of focus, I got out a piece of paper one night to make a list of the 'contenders' in each category.

In the 'pole dancer, or similar' category I had the following:

1. The girl from *Knocked Up* (I didn't know her name).
2. A girl who worked in a trendy coffee bar in London. She had served my brother and I the previous year (unfortunately, I hadn't actually spoken to her, didn't have her phone number and she lived on the other side of the world).
3. The personal trainer (female, obviously) from the first series of *The Biggest Loser*.
4. The blonde presenter from the Weather Channel (again, I didn't know her name).
5. A pole dancer who I had 'met' in *The Men's Gallery* a couple of years ago (we had briefly chatted, I knew her name was Sapphire, that she was only dancing to support her training as a vet and that she had a $50 note of mine—but again, I had no contact details). Mind you, I recall she seemed quite keen on me and had told me that I was

really handsome and sexy. And why wouldn't I believe her?

The list of contenders in the 'beautiful woman who loves children' category was a little more promising, but arguably more ambitious:

1. Cameron Diaz. Perfect. Defines the category completely.
2. Jennifer Hawkins. I truly felt there could be some karma here and maybe even a connection. Jen, as I like to call her, had once stood behind me while waiting to board a flight from Sydney to Melbourne. We had made brief eye contact and I was pretty sure that she had looked me up and down and smiled shyly. Even spookier, and more symbolically, I once got into a hotel lift with Ernie Dingo—weren't he and Jen on the same show, *Getaway*, or something? Were the Gods trying to tell me something?
3. Keira Knightly. I subsequently crossed her off the list as I wasn't sure how old she was and was worried about the risk of violating the 'must be over thirty' constraint. But I probably would have crossed her off anyway; who wants to go out with a girl who is better at soccer and taking free kicks than you are?
4. Mother Theresa. Was she married? Was she able to get married? Was she still alive?
5. A few girls from the office (names withheld). I wasn't sure whether they would all meet the 'must be over thirty' constraint either. I briefly wondered whether I could ask HR to do some kind of diversity survey across our female employees to determine age, marital status, interest in an older man, interest in an older man with asymmetrical testicles, views on children (love them, want them, have

them) and so on, to help me form a target market. But I knew in my heart that any early thirties, switched on, woman wouldn't be interested in me. They would want to make their own families, not get together with an old bloke with kids and slightly saggy pectorals.

The lists were fun for a while and my daughters both got quite good at identifying potential candidates. But the lists also revealed the rather unfortunate fact that I didn't actually know anyone who met my criteria. In my fantasies I was going to meet a woman who looked like Elle Macpherson, who loved me to bits, thought my children were wonderful (and in turn they would think that she was wonderful), came round when I wanted her to, knew when I needed alone time, went home when I wanted her to and wouldn't interfere with my family life. I knew she was out there somewhere, but I also knew that the chances of finding her were probably on the slim side.

So, where did this leave me in the real world? Most of the women in my social circle were, as expected, married or in long-term relationships. There were a couple who I quite liked and sort of fancied but it would clearly be inappropriate for me to make a move on them, plus they were all close to, or over, forty and I was hoping for someone a bit younger. There were also a few attractive single women in the office but I had already determined that they were unlikely to be interested in me, and I wasn't going to stoop so low as to be the senior executive preying on the youngsters with the promise of 'special training'. I had seen that kind of thing in a movie once, and it wasn't pretty. I suspected it might also be illegal.

The good news was that my analysis had led me to a conclusion, even though it wasn't a very promising one. The answer was not on my doorstep. I was going to need to meet some new people. This was both an exciting and daunting prospect. But where does a forty-five-year-old man with full-time child rearing responsibilities go to find a new woman? The answer, when it came, was obvious.

13

Girls on film

The good old World Wide Web! Why hadn't I thought of this before? It would be just like online shopping. I could do it from the safety of my own home and without the risk of embarrassing misunderstandings of the Sharni in Coles variety.

I had always been intrigued by the adverts that I noticed while I was online. You know the ones—the ones promising hundreds of local girls just waiting to meet (or similar) me. And didn't the girls in the adverts look great! They were sparkly, attractive and fun looking—and they wanted to be my friends! Truly my cup didst runneth over!

Having determined this was a good way forward, my first big decision was which site to join—it was a straight pick between the 'love and relationship' variety and the 'dating and no strings' variety. I decided to take the plunge and go 'dating and no strings'. In hindsight, this was akin to going to an Indian restaurant for the first time and asking for a vindaloo. It would certainly be hot, and more than a little bit painful. But at the time I was naive about the world of online dating—and believe me it truly is another world out there—I also felt that, given my current circumstances, I would be better suited to a 'no strings' type of relationship rather than a 'romance'. And besides, the 'no strings' girls looked a lot hotter.

There was a bit to do before the promised riches of the website would reveal themselves to me. Firstly, I had to complete my own profile. There were some basic questions to answer:

Age: I was forty-five and I wondered whether that might make me appear past it in cyber-sex land. I am quite a young looking bloke so I decided to re-invent myself as a forty-year-old. Then, in a moment of brilliant insight, I realised that a lot of women might view forty as a bit of a ceiling and only go for 'under 40s'. Rather conveniently, my brother was under forty at the time, so I simply adopted his date of birth, which made me a sprightly, yet, unrealistic, thirty-eight-year-old.

Height: I had to provide this information in centimetres and I am a feet and inches man. I knew I was five foot ten or eleven in the traditional measure but wasn't a hundred percent sure what that was in centimetres. I didn't want to make the mistake of going too short and appearing to be a dwarf, or of going too tall and appearing to be a basketball player. So I went to the trouble of using my calculator to work out my actual height in centimetres and plumped for the 1.8–1.9 metre category.

Weight: Easy. 73kg. I went for my pre-separation anxiety body mass because I didn't want my target market to think that I had the body of a fifteen-year-old.

Body Shape: This was a bit tricky. I knew I wasn't 'muscular' or 'cuddly' or even 'average'. But was I 'slim' or 'athletic'? I was in reasonable shape but I equated 'athletic' to representing the hard, toned body of a sportsman and probably someone under thirty, so I went for 'slim'. This turned out to be a mistake as I subsequently learnt that women equate 'slim' with 'weedy', but I didn't know this at the time.

Finally, I had to write a bit about myself and the type of relationship I was looking for. It wasn't too hard, particularly as I adopted something of my brother's personality into my profile—he's much cooler than me. I was quite pleased with the picture that I painted. I came across as someone who was caring and fun but with a passionate streak, looking for a regular relationship rather than just a one-night stand. I didn't want to position myself as just a shagger, I wanted, in consulting speak, a point of difference. Again, in hindsight, I had certainly achieved a point of difference. In the world of internet dating I had painted myself as Cliff Richard.

And then a moment that made me stop in my keyboard tracks. It was "strongly recommended" I added a photo to my profile. According to the website this would make it ten times more likely that I would find someone to have fun with. I thought about this for a while. I didn't have anything to hide but it was important for me to remain anonymous. What if one of my friends was on the site and saw my photo? Worse, what if a member of my family was on there and recognised me? Even worse, what if that family member was my mum—or my nan? I felt bad enough using elements of my brother's identity, interests and date of birth to put my profile together. How would I be able to explain this to my mum if she called me in shock, saying she had discovered that my brother, a married man, was using an internet dating site and, as the ultimate act of bad taste and betrayal, was using a photo of me in his profile?

But then again, if someone I knew (family members excepted) was also 'in the market' wouldn't that be an easy way to get together? And if they did come across my profile, how could they challenge me without also admitting that they too were an active internet dater?

It was tricky. But, despite the warning that the lack of a photo would significantly reduce my chances of an encounter, I decided to go without one. The other factor in my decision—and quite a major one—was that the only photo I had available was the one from my work security pass. This was a nice, smiley head and shoulders photo of me in my suit—not really the steely-eyed, sex-god look I needed. All my other photos were mostly holiday snaps of me and the kids. So, in the absence of an appropriately smouldering photo, I decided to rely on the cleverly crafted words in my profile to attract the fillies.

Hard work completed, it was time to search for my dream lady—or at least someone who seemed half decent. What would be my search criteria for finding Miss, or Mrs, Right? Or, more appropriately, Miss, or Mrs, Right Up For It. It was quite simple, using the guidance of the site I went for:

Age: 25–35 (on the basis there was likely to be some significant understatement going on).

Body shape: Slim or athletic. I was tempted to add 'average' but I prefer slim women, so went with that.

Marital status: Any. I felt a bit bad about this. But I wasn't looking for a long-term relationship or to tempt a married woman away from her husband and I thought it might make things a bit easier if she also had commitments.

Ethnic Origin: This was becoming more and more like a work-based diversity survey. I didn't want to appear to have a racial bias so I went for Caucasian. I reconciled this on the basis that I was dismissing all other forms of ethnicity equally.

Attractiveness: Another difficult one. I went for 'very' rather than 'above average'. Why not? I, rather naively, wanted someone hot.

Photo: Hell yeah! I wanted to see what I was getting into. My own lack of photo nagged at me—but again, I was sure that my clever words would act as the perfect babe magnet.

I pressed the submit button and waited while the computer compiled my new love life. Twenty seconds later I had fifteen matches! Naturally, I immediately went to the profiles with photos and ignored all the clever words their owners had written about themselves (it's okay, the irony wasn't lost on me). I discounted a number of the contenders, as they didn't appear to be my type. I then discounted a few more because, although they had attached a photo, it was either a close up shot of their intimate parts (call me a prude, but I found that a bit disconcerting), or a photo of a woman—supposedly the profile owner—engaging in an act that a gymnast would be proud of. Far too out there for me.

Sadly this culling left me with only five suitable profiles. I sent each of them a nice little message along the lines of how much their profile interested me and how I would like to see more of them. A bit cheeky I thought—but, in reality, it just made me look even more like Cliff Richard.

I spent the next week checking my mailbox on an hourly basis for replies. I had two. One from the system administrator, welcoming me to the website and wishing me luck with my searching, and another, also from the system administrator, suggesting I pay more money and upgrade to Gold membership. This would provide me with access to more specific search criteria, making it more likely that I would find a suitable match.

A month later, despite more searches and more messages, I had nothing. Twenty-dollars down the drain. Something needed to be done; it was embarrassing to be continually ignored by all the women on the site. So, in the second month of my quest for love, I changed my approach. I widened my search criteria to include people without photos and people who rated themselves 'average body shape' and 'average attractiveness'. I was now on a mission. All I wanted was one miserable, sodding message in recognition that I existed.

My new, more inclusive, approach brought a lot more

candidates into the net but it also brought with it a lot of new challenges. It was all very well reading profiles of people describing themselves as attractive but, without a photo to look at, how was I to know whether they were—and if their view of attractiveness matched mine? After all, I was hoping to meet the girl of my (hot) dreams and I wanted to know what she looked like.

However, my musings were all a bit academic as, regardless of the wider search criteria, I was still no further forward. The only person sending me messages was my good friend the system administrator. I did think about sending him/her a note asking for a photo, seeing as they were so happy to communicate with me.

Another month wasted but this time the management consultant in me took over. I needed to know what I was dealing with—it was time for some fact-based analysis, as we say in the trade. So I did the only thing I thought to be logical—I set myself up on the site as a female. It wasn't too hard. I basically put together a profile of the type of woman that I was looking for minus the photo, for obvious reasons. I know, highly unethical, but justifiable as part of a project to assess the market.

The results were quite interesting. As a slim, attractive woman without a photo I was attracting two or three messages a day, mostly from men without photos, and varying from the very simple "Hi, message me" to the more creative, where the boys told me how good I looked (quite how they managed to reach that conclusion I wasn't sure), or what they wanted to do to me.

The next step was to up the ante. I added a photo of a reasonably attractive woman to my profile (I can't admit to where I got the photo from). The impact was astounding. I went from two to three messages a day to around fifteen. So this was what my target market was experiencing—a flood of people contacting them. If I were a girl, I imagined that the only way to deal with all these messages efficiently would be to delete all those without a photo and all those that were just a few single words, or crass. I was tempted to reply to a few of the more inane messages that I received and pretend to be interested, but it was getting far too weird already—and I didn't want to fuel the fantasies of complete strangers.

Despite feeling as though I had cheated my fellow man, my cross-gender internet dating experiment had taught me something very valuable. If I was to be successful, I needed to stand out from the mass of messages that the girls on the site were receiving—and that meant I had no choice but to have a photo to go with my words of seduction. But which photo? I looked at my collection of happy snaps stored on the computer. Me with the kids; me with the wife; me with my mum; me pulling a stupid face. None of them ranked with the better photos I had received as a 'woman', which were of men out having fun, chilling in a bar or sitting in the sun without a shirt on. Funnily enough, my domestic, happily married photos were not suitable for a dating site.

The photo, or lack of photo, issue was tricky. What look should I go for? Should I smile and look normal or go for something a bit hotter? And could I do hot? Should I focus on my face or display a bit of my body? If so, which bit? What should I wear? More clothes or fewer clothes? A lot of blokes went for the open shirt look, or tight T-shirt and big arms look. I didn't think this would suit me; I've got the arms of a young David Bowie. In the end I decided on a mysterious, cool look. In my mind's eye this was the look David Beckham adopts when he is lining up a free kick, or advertising designer aftershave or shades. One eyebrow partially raised, eyes slightly squint, staring at the horizon with just a hint of "yeah, I know I'm hotter than you—fucker". I thought that look would suit me just nicely.

Having decided on my look, the next challenge was how to capture it. It would be a little hard to explain to one of the children, or to a friend, why I needed a David Beckham-esq photo, and even more embarrassing to put them behind the camera and witness my efforts to capture it. So I tried the self-portrait route. Children seem to have the natural ability to hold a camera, point it at themselves and get a perfectly framed self-portrait. I failed miserably. In the end I went back to the old fashioned self-timer approach, set the camera up on a pile of books, pressed the shutter, ran round to my mark and adopted my pose. Although this approach resulted in a dramatic improvement in my framing capability, the downside of the self-timer was that I had to hold my pose for five seconds or so, which may not seem a long time—but it's an age when you are trying to hold a 'dangerous' look.

An hour later, I sat at my computer looking at the fruits of my labours and realised, rather despondently, that my efforts weren't good. I seemed to have a gift for creating a range of looks that might be useful for getting me a role in a B-grade comedy about nerdy kids, but not a look that was going to score me some hot bird. My range of looks covered:

1. Man who needs glasses (excessive squint).
2. Man who has had a nasty shock (excessive eyebrow elevation).
3. Man who needs a poo (excessive grimace and pout).
4. Man who has just had a poo (double eyebrow raise, too relaxed).

5. Man who is pissed off with the whole process (no attempt at trying anything).

I deleted the lot. I was trying to be someone I wasn't. I couldn't compete with Becks or the hundreds of young tradies out there on the website.

So I did what I probably should have done at the beginning. I went through my normal photos, found one where I was largely on my own, and cropped myself out of it. It wasn't a great photo but at least it proved that I had two arms, two legs and a reasonable smile. The other redeeming feature of the photo was that it didn't actually look too much like me, so anyone I knew who might be 'browsing' my profile would have to look hard to discover my secret.

Feeling a bit better, I went about sending my messages hoping that I had improved my chances of a response.

14

I want you to want me

Two weeks after posting my photo I had my first reply from someone other than the system administrator—and I was terrified. What do I do now, I thought? Suppose this mystery woman was a psycho, determined to wreak revenge on mankind following some disastrous relationship or hideous attempt to rough her up by some bloke she had met on the internet. Even worse, suppose 'she' was a man (after all I had pulled that trick). To add to my doubts, she was a respondent from the outer range of my selection criteria i.e. average attractiveness, average body shape and no photo. But, at the end of the day, the message was articulate and, most importantly, it was the only message that I had. And it was positive, she liked my profile and photo (!) and wanted to know more about me.

Having come this far I decided that sending a reply couldn't hurt. So I told her a bit about myself and what I did for a living—how interesting that must have been. Next day, to my amazement, she had also replied telling me about what she did for a living (event management), that she was sick of internet dating time wasters, that she never sent out a photo of herself in case one of her clients recognised her and, to my surprise, included her mobile number. I looked at the number for a long time. It was only a number and yet it made the mystery woman, and the whole situation, a lot more real. Scary! There were no instructions as to what I should do with her number and, because I was an internet virgin, I didn't know what the next step was supposed to be. Was this an invitation to call her? I thought about it for a while and decided not to call as this would involve giving my own number away. Plus, I half expected a bloke with a deep, gruff voice to answer.

But the dilemma and fear of action nagged away at me. I did nothing for a day and then, after a couple of beers for Dutch courage, sent her a note asking if she would like to meet up. She didn't like time wasters after all—so best to cut to the chase. In an act of faith I also sent her my own mobile number. A few hours later she raised the stakes and replied with a text and, after some increasingly flirtatious messaging, we agreed to meet—a massive and intimidating step forward. She was going to be in the city the following week and so we arranged that the first step in our journey of discovery would take place at a coffee shop close to my office.

On the morning of the meeting I was pretty much crapping my pants. What had I got myself into? Was I placing myself at risk? Or was I just being a girl—after all we were meeting in the middle of the day, in a coffee shop, in full public view. What could possibly go wrong? I needed to get a grip. I was the man and she was the girl (or at least I hoped she was), so shouldn't she be the one feeling nervous? I had a pretty difficult morning at work and found it hard to get anything done, but it was too late for second thoughts, five minutes before the meeting time she sent me a text to say that she was outside the coffee shop. Off I went like a little boy on his first day of school—and just like then I wished that my mum was with me to hold my hand.

As I approached the coffee shop I saw a woman with long blonde hair standing with her back to me. I was a bit confused. There was no other woman in sight, and this was definitely the right coffee shop. The woman standing before me, there is no other way to put this, was a little on the large side. In fact, I would go as far as saying that she was big. Now I have nothing against larger women, it's just that her profile described her body shape as 'average'. This girl might have been average if she was on a bus trip with a group of middle-aged American tourists, but I was pretty sure that she wasn't average within the population of twenty-five–thirty-five-year-olds from Melbourne. I'll say it again—I have nothing against the overweight but if I was looking to buy a car and, having found an advert for a VW Golf and driven across Melbourne to look at it, had arrived to find the owner proudly showing me his Ford Territory, I think I could rightly feel a bit pissed off. After all, it's not what it says on the tin.

Still, maybe I was wrong. Perhaps the girl I was meeting was standing in the shadow of the larger lady and I just couldn't see her yet. A form of solar eclipse. In a moment the planets would re-align and my averagely attractive, average body shaped, internet correspondent would be revealed. But no, I was right the first time; this larger lady was, in fact, my date. I smiled as we shook hands trying not to look disappointed. To make matters worse she was tall and towered over me in a most disconcerting way. I hadn't picked up on the height from her profile either.

We had a coffee and made small talk. I know this sounds awful, but I wasn't really interested as I was still trying to get over this outrageous breach of the Trade Practices Act. So I listened while she told me about her job (can't remember much, I'm afraid); how boys loved her eyes (which I had to admit were quite striking, although she kept widening them for emphasis in a way that was slightly disturbing); how boys loved her boobs, which she felt were her best feature (they were huge—you would need a map to find your way around them); how she didn't send out photos of herself for fear of being recognised (is that the real reason, I thought?); and that her name wasn't June. For one hideous moment, I thought she was going to compound my misery by telling me her name was Alan, but it turned out that her name was Jane-clever bit of vowel swapping. Very smart!

I was beginning to feel like Simon Cowell suffering through a poor *Pop Idol* or *X-Factor* audition. I knew from the first moment that this was a non-starter and I was getting really tense inside. I wanted to blurt out "and exactly which part of your body would you describe as average" but, rather than exploding and being brutal à la Simon Cowell, I did the right thing and listened politely, nodding occasionally, and offering the odd word of encouragement—I bit like when you're talking with your mad granny. I came over all Cliff Richardy again. Was I being a bastard? She was probably a nice enough girl—I just felt that I had been duped.

Eventually the coffee cups were emptied and the conversation, hers not mine, came to a natural close. What was supposed to happen next? I explained that this was my first (and possibly last) internet date and apologised for not knowing the protocol. Terror gripped my guts. Supposing she widened her eyes and replied that it was my responsibility to have the hotel room booked and to whisk her away for an hour of passion—the naked wrestling scene from the *Borat* movie flooded my mind. So I quickly added that, unfortunately, I had to get back to the office.

To my relief she suggested we both go away and think about whether we wanted to see each other again. I suspect I agreed to this rather too readily. I felt like an eight-year-old boy with itchy pants who has just got an Action Man for Christmas and wants to run away from the rest of the family to play with it. I gratefully returned to the safety and security of my office, walking far too quickly and dodging down side streets in case I was being followed. Once I was through reception and into the lifts I breathed a huge sigh of relief.

The following day I sent June/Jane a polite email saying how much I had enjoyed meeting her, but that internet dating wasn't for me. I was a bit worried that she would bombard my mobile with abusive messages but I never heard from her again. There is obviously a degree of honour amongst internet daters.

Still, at least I was off the mark. Despite the disappointment, it had been a good learning experience and had reinforced to me that internet dating was a murky old world, driven by misstatement, and that I shouldn't take anything at face value. Time to tighten my search and go back to my original criteria focussed on slim, attractive girls—and definitely only those with a photo.

The other good news was that my own photo was starting to pay dividends. Within a week I had made contact with another girl who seemed to be quite promising. She had a photo, was actually quite attractive and appeared to be genuinely on the slim side. I was a lot more confident second time around and, having got to the exchange of mobile numbers phase, I asked if I could give her a call. We had a couple of short conversations and agreed to meet one evening after work, in a bar in the city.

I got to the bar early, ordered a drink and waited. This time I knew what my target lady looked like and if she had the software that they use on *NCIS* to 'age' photos she would also have a rough idea of what I looked like. Finding each other and meeting up shouldn't be too hard. Five minutes after the allotted meeting time she sent me a text to say that she would be arriving soon. I fixed my gaze on the doorway and was a little confused when a woman, who looked a bit like the girl in the photo, came into the bar, scanned the room, made eye contact with me and walked over. My first thought was that 'Vicky', the name she had given me, had sent her older sister, or maybe even her mum, to let me know that she wouldn't be able to make our date. But no, this was Vicky. A fair bit older than her photo suggested but still attractive, with a slim top half although quite a large bum which, again, hadn't been apparent from the photo. But, on balance, given my previous experience I wasn't too disappointed. I was with Meatloaf on this one— 'two out of three ain't bad'.

She was actually quite good fun. She was a nurse and had some funny stories about men she had met who weren't quite what they had made themselves out to be (a lot of them were married apparently—fancy that!). She was a serial internet dater and had a number of different profiles, on different sites, to attract a variety of men. Quite complicated, but interesting— see, it's a whole new world.

It was all going well until I mentioned my children. I was proud of being a single parent and I assumed she would be so impressed by my dedication to my girls that this new information would cement a situation that was already going swimmingly and pave the way for a couple of positive base movements. Tragically, it had the opposite effect. She was adamant that, despite clearly being very free with her favours (and believe me, she was very free), she didn't 'do' men with kids as it made things too complicated. Her logic was that men with kids weren't as available as she needed them to be and, because there were so many men out there, she could afford to stick to her principles—even if it meant letting a few good ones slip through the net. And in this instance, despite the fact she liked me, I was going to slip through the net.

Knowing that I wasn't going to get 'done' changed the tone of the evening and actually took the pressure off. We ended up having a relaxed, fun night and were having a great time and, after a couple more drinks, I asked her to be my internet dating coach and to guide me through the game—because it is a game.

It was a fascinating night and when it was time to go, I plucked up the courage to ask her the one question that was still going round and round in my head.

"Hypothetically, if I didn't have kids, would you want to get funky with me?" I asked.

"Yes, I think it would be fun," she replied, without even hesitating.

"So why don't we? I can find some free time. It just needs to be planned."

"Because I don't do men with kids."

"No exceptions?"

"No exceptions."

We shared a cab, I dropped her off at her apartment, still hoping there might be a last minute change of heart, but sadly not, she wished me luck and simply gave me a kiss on the cheek. And so I headed home.

It was disappointing, but I consoled myself with the facts that (i) I was 'doable', apart from an unbreakable principle that prevented the actual act from occurring, and (ii) I now had fantastic insight into a woman's view of internet dating which I could use to my advantage. I was still an internet dating virgin, but only due to a technicality.

I was ready to get out there and get busy, armed with my new knowledge and confidence. But then something happened that rendered my need for the internet redundant.

15

Something about you

My internet dating experience had not been successful in terms of achieving my ultimate goal i.e. having a rumble with a complete stranger and, in hindsight, I'm sure this was a good thing. But my experiences had not been a complete waste of time. I had been on two blind dates, I had taken my first tentative steps back into the world of single, or allegedly single, women and, as a result, my confidence was sky high. After all, I had been told by an experienced female shagger that I was 'doable'. We may not have actually 'done it' but in a strange way I felt as though I was now back in the saddle.

It was a good feeling, in fact it was similar to the feeling that I had as a seventeen-year-old when I was surprisingly selected for the school's first XI cricket team (there must have been an outbreak of cholera across both the senior and junior schools for me to get picked). Unfortunately the match was abandoned due to the weather but I felt justified in claiming that I was a first team player, even if I had spent all day sitting in the pavilion watching the rain. Applying these same principles, I was satisfied that I now qualified as a fully paid up member of the internet shaggers club—albeit a non-practicing member. A sort of Cliff Richard-style member.

However, the winds of change were getting ready to blow

and they would bring my days of internet dating and my Cliff Richard persona to an end. It was a simple and inauspicious thing; I received an invite to a drinks party for the Year 6 school parents. When we were married, my wife and I used to go to a whole range of school events religiously and I normally found them a bit of a bind. Lots of people I didn't really know, talking about how well their kids were doing at netball and brass rubbing. As I have said before, I'm not naturally sociable.

So my first reaction on getting this invite was to forget about it. My other issue was that I was still uncomfortable about going to a social event that my wife, and worse her soul mate, could be at. I wasn't yet ready to be in the same location as them, particularly when it involved a relatively intimate evening. But the main reason for my ignoring the invite was that this was a school parents' drinks party and none of the Year 6 mothers met my 'ideal woman' criteria. How could they when by default they all had children? It would hardly be a happy hunting ground for a horny hobbit like me.

But I was wrong, completely and utterly wrong. Right up there on the scale of wrongness with the referee who disallowed Frank Lampard's goal for England against Germany in the 2010 World Cup. Life changingly wrong in fact because, although I didn't know it at the time, at this party I would meet the woman who I would go on to marry. And I certainly didn't expect that.

Annabel, who was in Year 6, asked me if I would be going to the drinks. I think in some ways the kids get more excited about these things than the parents. She was disappointed when I told her I wouldn't be and, to my surprise, became quite insistent that I go because she wanted me to get out and get social again. She was unaware that I had already had a couple of cracks at getting out and getting social again, but I let that pass.

Annabel went through my wardrobe and selected a shirt for me. It was touching and she was right. I couldn't hide from my friends, and life, forever. I was still a coward though, and sent my wife a text saying that I wanted to go to the drinks but wouldn't do if she was planning on being there. She replied that she was happy not to go if it made me feel uncomfortable. I immediately wished I had been stronger; it was pathetic asking for permission to go out.

Still, I felt good when I arrived at the party. My friends seemed genuinely pleased to see me and Annabel was right, I enjoyed talking to people, telling them what I had been up to and how I was coping. I even managed to laugh about some of the unfortunate situations I had been through.

About an hour into the party I caught sight of someone who I had not seen before. She was standing near me while I was talking to someone else (sorry that someone else, I have no idea who you were). I was struck by her pretty face and then doubly struck when she smiled. She possessed a great, feel-good smile and I will never forget seeing it for the first time. The picture is still frozen in my mind.

Instantaneously, my internet dating training kicked in and I became a steely-faced hunter, or at least as much as a steely-faced hunter as it is possible to be when dressed in a pastel pink shirt. I was still talking to the 'someone else', so I needed to be furtive. I began running through my checklist.

Step One: Check marital status. I had a discrete look at the fourth finger of her left hand. There was a ring on it—a strange, metallic, funky thing—certainly not an engagement or wedding ring. Interesting. I wasn't entirely sure what this sort of ring signified, maybe some form of commitment, or maybe she was a lesbian. But would a lesbian be at a party for Year 6 parents? Regardless, I was pretty sure she wasn't married. Step One: Pass.

I momentarily lost focus on my pursuit because I couldn't drop the lesbian idea. She was quite pretty and not at all butch. I subtly scanned the party for another unmarried woman and evidence of a potential lesbian relationship. Amazingly, in the corner there was another attractive female who looked as though she wasn't wearing a wedding ring either. Could it be? In the middle of the suburbs? But why would two lesbians be at a Year 6 parents' party? How would they qualify? Surely one of them must have had a child to justify their invitation? Maybe the lesbian thing was only recent and one of them had previously been married? So was one, or both of them, bisexual?

I was now way off track and rapidly disappearing into full-on fantasyland. A lesbian, a bisexual and me, and we weren't making polite conversation. My celibate months hit me hard, quite literally. I felt my chest tighten and I think I may have unfortunately let out a little involuntary groan. I was in real danger; my baby bat brain had taken over my real brain.

"Focus," I muttered to myself.

"Sorry?" The someone I was talking to asked.

I think we were in the middle of a conversation about the merits of young boys wearing skullcaps when they played football.

"It's all about focus," I emphasised, for clarification. "Success in any team sport is a question of focus."

"You're right. Focus is critical."

I think I had got away with it. We were both agreed about the importance of focus in team sports, we were just thinking about completely different team sports. I excused myself. I needed to continue with my checklist and move onto step two.

15 Something about you

Step Two: Check physical equipment. I had a discrete look from the side. Petite, not excessively tall (okay, a little on the short side), dark hair and definitely pretty in a Shania Twain sort of way. I had a discrete look from the back. Narrow waist, curvy rear end. She seemed a suitable candidate for rumpy pumpy. All good. Step Two: Pass.

Step Three: Check personality. This was a more difficult step as it involved conversation. My inner voice started to speak to me. Don't be nervous. Trust in your internet training. Isolate your prey and move in quickly and purposefully. Remember you're 'doable'. Don't be scared of rejection. What's the worst that could happen? I told my inner voice to shut up; I was worried that my lips might be silently mouthing the words of my inner monologue. I also realised that I was now standing on my own. Maybe I had actually been thinking out loud and muttering to myself and so had been given a wide berth by the other party guests, as if I was the local nutter on the bus. I glanced around with the furtive look of a schoolboy who has just nicked a bar of chocolate from the corner shop. It was okay. No one appeared to have noticed.

I decided to play for time and headed to the bar for a top up, and from where I would have a better vantage point—all the while keeping my eyes on the target. And then it happened. She began talking to a friend of mine. The perfect opportunity for me to move in.

"Hi Samantha," I said to our mutual friend. "Haven't seen you for ages. How are you?"

I tried to appear nonchalant, although my target remained in the corner of my eye.

"I'm well. Great to see you too." And a second later. "Do you know Alison?"

Bingo. I turned to say hello and shake hands. A momentary

mental flash of entwined limbs, some of which I think belonged to me, passed through my head; but my improper thoughts were immediately doused by that killer smile and her big, brown eyes. Target acquired, I was locked on.

We seemed to end up speaking to each other for the rest of the night. We had a lot in common. We had both lost our dads within a few weeks of each other, her eldest son and my youngest daughter were in the same class at school and she had been divorced for eight years and lived on her own. I told her I was separated, just in case she thought that I was coming on to her inappropriately, but I needn't have worried about that as she had also noticed me. She had never seen me at a school event before and was interested to know who I was—and even more interested when she was told that I was on my own. I politely resisted the temptation to ask about the strange ring on her finger or her sexuality, it seemed a bit early for that.

By about one o'clock in the morning most people had left the party. We were still talking. I can't remember all the details but I do remember that Alison spent a long time listening to me and not interrupting or talking over me. I wasn't used to this as most of the women I know are natural talkers. It was refreshing to drive the conversation for a change. Sadly I now know this was a one-off—and that Alison's mouth must have been a bit off colour that night.

She told me she had grown up in Whyalla. I had no idea where this was, but apparently it's a small town in South Australia. She also told me that, in the early 1980s, she held the title of Miss Whyalla. I was impressed. Here I was talking to a former beauty queen.

The hosts of the party had now changed into their pyjamas and were making a hot milk drink, so it seemed a bit rude to stay any longer. We shook hands again and said our goodbyes.

No exchange of phone numbers, no awkward "can I see you again?". We didn't need to. We both knew that we would be at our children's Year 6 graduation in two weeks time and would have the opportunity to continue talking then. I went home happy. I had a nice, warm feeling that I had met someone new who I was attracted to, knowing I was looking forward to seeing her again and wondering whether I would get to shag her. Stage Three: Pass. Checklist complete.

The next morning I did a bit of research into Whyalla. It's a very small place. Apparently, in the year Alison was the reigning Miss Whyalla the total population of the town was just a few thousand people. Only five women aged between eighteen and twenty-five entered the competition that year. Of those five, three were previous winners and therefore ineligible, and a fourth was also ineligible due to 'inappropriate gender'. So that basically left Alison to romp home unopposed. I further discovered that the Miss Whyalla competition is actually about fundraising and the title is awarded to the person who raises the most money for charity. This was a worthy cause no doubt, but it meant that I hadn't spent the evening with a former beauty queen after all, just someone who was good at rattling a can.

I also found out, rather gratuitously, that 80 percent of the male population of Whyalla enjoy having sex in the shower. The other 20 percent haven't been to prison yet.

Over the two weeks before I hoped to see Alison again I began to understand a little of what my wife must have felt when she was embarking on her affair, except I didn't have the fear of being caught hanging over me. The anticipation of talking to Alison again and the excitement of a potential relationship were intoxicating. I felt ten times better about myself. I was happy; I was confident; I had more energy. The possibilities seemed endless and as a consequence I felt younger. I was in danger of acting like a teenager.

My old counsellor had described as 'pointless' my futile attempts to talk rationally to my wife when she was in the process of leaving me. He told me that when someone is in love the chemicals in their brain are similar to those present in someone who has been drinking or is on drugs. This makes it impossible to talk to them logically as they are effectively drunk, they won't listen and they won't be rational. I wasn't in love, but I now understood a little of what he meant.

The next time I saw Alison was, as I had anticipated, at the Year 6 graduation after-party. It was packed. I had two dilemmas. The first was to find and talk to Alison without making it too obvious and the second was to avoid my wife, who was circulating through the crowd. It wasn't easy. I had a number of conversations in which I wasn't properly engaged while my eyes patrolled the room. The evening was passing quickly and, although I had achieved the objective of avoiding my wife, I still hadn't managed to corner Alison. I was getting tense, if I didn't speak to her tonight would I get another opportunity?

Finally, with only half an hour of the event remaining, I managed to spy her in a relatively open space and, dodging the crowds, I moved towards her. Unfortunately, with perfectly crap timing, one of my friends intercepted us and innocently and enthusiastically started talking about rugby and his forthcoming family holiday to the UK. I desperately wanted him to leave us alone.

And then an opportunity—my friend mentioned he would be departing on the 1am flight that evening. I had to seize the moment. I decided to tell a lie. Just a little one.

"As I was driving here I heard on the radio there's a big fog bank over the north of Melbourne," I said. "People are being advised to allow more time for car journeys, particularly those heading to the airport."

"Really? That's a pain," he replied, looking a little perplexed. "Fog in the summer? That's very unusual."

"Yeah. I'm pretty sure that's what they said."

I was feeling a bit guilty. He would find out eventually that my fog story wasn't true. Still, it's always a good idea to leave plenty of time when going to the airport.

"I'd better be off," he concluded. "I don't want to miss my flight." And he disappeared back into the crowd, in search of his wife.

"Drive carefully," I offered, as a farewell greeting.

My mate has never subsequently said anything about the mysterious fog bank. Presumably he was just glad that it didn't affect his trip to the airport.

The evening was almost over but I finally had some time with Alison and we picked up from where we had left off two weeks earlier. It was so easy and natural. However we only had fifteen minutes before it was time to go, and there was no forthcoming event at which we would cross paths. I knew I wanted to see her again, which meant that I had no choice but to ask her out on a date. Unfortunately, I only knew how to do this by email or text; my internet dating training hadn't covered asking someone out face to face. We walked to the door with the crowd. With every step I was running out of time, but I was hemmed in by our group of friends, who also wanted to talk to Alison or me.

Suddenly we were in the school playground. In my youth I had asked many girls out in the playground, or at least asked them to join me behind the oak tree, and so I took this as a sign. I stopped walking and she stopped walking—and so I asked her.

Or more precisely, as calmly as I could, although in reality it was a tad rushed, I said something like "Umwouldyouliketogoforadrinksometime."

"Sure," she replied.

I had nothing else to say. I had used up all my energy on the opening line.

"Okay," I replied. "I'll give you a call."

I already had her number—that's what the class list was for.

16

Blame it on the moon

My date with Alison was going well. We were sitting in a cosy wine bar, drinking a nice glass of red and talking about all sorts of things. We talked about ourselves, our families, the hard times we had been through and the things that made us happy. We both agreed our lives had been difficult recently and that we needed to have more fun. The chemistry was good, so good in fact that I plucked up the courage to ask her about the funky ring on the fourth finger of her left hand. She was silent for a moment.

"It's a commitment ring," she said slowly, looking into her wine glass.

"Oh," I replied.

It was all I could think of. I was hoping that I hadn't made the mistake of being too personal too soon. But she continued, very hesitantly.

"It's not what you think. I have a special friend. We met a few years ago and we became close." She was slowly twisting the wine glass in her fingers, still not looking up. "She's a lot younger than me, a dancer. She lost her way for a while and we became friends. She means a lot to me."

"Oh," I said again. My vocabulary was taking a short holiday.

"To be honest with you it's largely a sexual relationship. It's very intense." She was still speaking slowly and couldn't look me in the eye.

Oh my God—she was a lesbian after all. I had nothing to say. She was still talking.

"I haven't been with a man for a long time, and to be honest I miss it. I want to experience it again."

Oh my God—so she *was* bisexual. I still had nothing to say. And she was still talking.

"My special friend has never even been with a man. We have talked about it from time to time. I'm trying to encourage her. I think she would like it."

She looked up at me with those big brown eyes. "I would like you to meet her. You could be so good for her—so good for both of us really." She held my eye and wet her lips nervously.

My breath caught and my heart was pounding. My internet training hadn't covered this eventuality. What next? The waitress came over to ask if we wanted another drink. As I turned to look up, the waitress started to slowly spin and transformed gracefully into a fox. The tabletop opened, revealing a dark passage, which I was sucked into, and I began to fall down a long, earthy tunnel. I remember the light fading and then, nothing.

I woke up with a start. It was four in the morning. The house was quiet. I was a bit sweaty but otherwise everything was all right. I took a deep breath and calmed myself down. I slept fitfully until morning.

*

The evening of my first date with Alison had arrived. I was looking forward to seeing her again and was partly nervous, partly excited. Our respective Year 6 children were going to a break-up party so we agreed to meet there, drop our kids off and go for a quick drink before pick up time. As I drove up, I thought I saw Alison sitting in her car. I parked, Annabel jumped out with a hurried goodbye, and I moved my car behind what I assumed to be Alison's car. It was a dark and rainy night so, rather than banging on her car window and risking frightening her, I decided to give her a call.

"Hello," said a voice. It didn't sound like Alison, a bit older and maybe a bit gruffer. But it was her number, so I carried on. Maybe she had a cold.

"I think I'm parked behind you. Do you drive a white CRV? Would you like me to get into your car?"

"Sorry?" said the voice. "Who is this?"

I pulled the phone from my ear. According to my phone I had called Alison, but unfortunately I had called her home number rather than her mobile. I had no idea who I was speaking with.

"Sorry. My mistake. Wrong number." I hung up.

Shit. Not a good start. Probably scared the babysitter.

I started again, this time being very careful to ring her mobile number. It was engaged and went straight to voicemail. This was turning into a disaster.

I waited, not quite sure of my next move. But then my phone rang. It was Alison—mobile rather than home—she confirmed that she drove a white CRV and agreed that I should get into her car so we could head off. She told me that she had just received a call from her mum, who had been very confused by a strange phone call from a bloke who claimed to be parked behind her. Her mum was worried that Alison was being stalked by some sicko, particularly as Alison had said she was dropping in to see a girlfriend that evening. Alison was now feeling guilty she had told her mum a little lie and had confessed to meeting me instead. All in all a bit awkward for everyone, but hopefully something that could be dismissed as just a little misunderstanding.

We made our way to a cosy wine bar and sat there drinking a nice glass of red and talking about all sorts of things. We talked about ourselves, our families, the hard times we had been through and the things that made us happy. We both agreed our lives had been difficult recently and that we needed to have more fun. The chemistry was good, so good in fact that I plucked up the courage to ask her about the funky ring on the fourth finger of her left hand. She was silent for a moment.

"It's a commitment ring," she said slowly, looking into her wine glass.

"Oh," I replied. It was all I could think of. I was having a strange case of *déjà vu*.

"It's not what you think," she continued, slowly twisting the wine glass in her fingers, still not looking up.

I didn't think she could be so sure of that. My mind was racing and I was thinking all kinds of things. What was she going to say next? I looked at the waitress, no sign of a graceful transformation into a fox this time.

"I've been seeing someone for a few years," she said slowly, choosing her words carefully. "We used to live together but we don't anymore."

"Is it a man?" I asked, nervously.

"Of course," she said laughing. "Why, do I look like a lesbian?"

"No of course not, but you never know in this modern world," I exclaimed far too loudly and then started to laugh rather too hysterically. I was making a horrible, machine gun like, 'ha-ha-ha-ha' sound. I'm sure that I looked, and sounded, like a right twat.

Alison studied me, quizzically. Did she think I was a right

twat? This was a very personal conversation and I was acting like a kookaburra on speed.

"It's been quite a serious, but difficult, relationship and I've been thinking of ending it for a while. He lives in Adelaide. I'm sort of single."

So, it was all on the table. Despite the commitment ring she had effectively told me that she was ready to think about moving on and trying something new. I think we both knew that this moment signalled the start of something, we just didn't know what.

It was pouring when we left the wine bar and we only had one umbrella between us. This forced us to walk closer together than was normal and our arms occasionally touched, giving me a little jolt of excitement each time. We drove back to the break-up party and said our goodbyes. Alison had visitors over Christmas and was then going away for the New Year. It turned out that her 'serious but difficult' relationship was coming to visit her, so we wouldn't be able to meet up again until January.

That was fine by me. I was prepared to take things slowly. Neither of us was in a rush, and Alison had an existing relationship to resolve.

17

Happy Xmas (war is over)

Christmas 2007. It was going to be a Christmas unlike any other.

I have to admit that I'm a big fan of Christmas. It's not because I like to celebrate the birth of Jesus and reflect on the event that paved the way to everlasting life, it's actually because I have a more traditional view of Christmas—for me it's all about family, good food and drink, and presents.

I have a whole set of great Christmases locked away in my mind. My earliest memories are of being a child and waking up in the dark on a cold English morning to attack my stocking; then, as I grew older, memories of long lunches that finished after dark, *Morecambe and Wise* on Christmas Day and a Roger Moore/Bond film on Boxing Day; and then, when I had my own family, memories of loading the car for a three-hour trip across the stark, frozen country to spend a few days with my mum and dad, being completely pampered and sharing in their joy of spending time with their grandchildren.

My last Christmas in the UK involved renting a farmhouse in Devon with my wife and my girls, my parents, my brother, my sister and her children, and my nan. It was all log fires, long walks, mince pies and sherry—and I loved it. Christmas just seems to work better in the northern hemisphere—the dark, the cold and the general misery of winter are broken by the bright beacon of light and warmth that is Christmas.

Perhaps because of my childhood memories I have always struggled slightly with Christmas in Australia. The sun, the barbeque and the traditional routing of the English cricket team were initially a little hard to get used to, but over the years I have adapted to the change in environment and Christmas has once again become a time for family. Our typical Australian Christmas involved either going up to the humidity of Brisbane to stay with my wife's parents, elements of her family braving the trip to Melbourne (despite the calls of "why would you want to go there?") and, occasionally, my mum and dad coming out from the UK. My dad was also a Christmas traditionalist so his arrival would be the cue for us to sweat our way through the production of a very English, and generally very inappropriate, Delia Smith Christmas lunch of turkey, chipolatas, roast potatoes and plum pudding served with brandy butter.

So, as our first Christmas as a threesome approached, I began to get a little apprehensive and could feel myself mourning the family life that had gone forever. This would also be the first Christmas for me and the rest of my UK family without my dad. It was going to be a painful time, particularly for my mum and my sister, who were missing him desperately. Part of me wanted to be with them at Christmas, to share both in the sorrow and the happy memories.

Christmas was also going to be a painful time for me and the girls. I couldn't think of anything better representing the end of the family life that we had enjoyed and valued, than the three of us sitting around the dinner table on our own. But I didn't want to get the girls down with my melancholy thoughts—it was Christmas after all—and, despite everything that had happened, they were still getting excited.

We planned our big day—or at least the food part of it. Roast chicken (one of the few things I could cook well), which I intended to embellish with some sausages wrapped in bacon, followed by Sara Lee sticky date toffee pudding. A little bit different to our previous Christmases, and certainly short on the additional trimmings, but the girls were happy, at least on the surface.

My planning was thrown in the air by my wife.

"It will be Christmas in December," she told me, as part of a phone call about something else.

"You don't say," I replied, rather annoyingly I have to admit. "Whose idea was that? When is it normally Christmas?"

"Very funny. I don't want our difficulties to spoil the girls' Christmas. It's a family time after all."

I almost hung up. I had come to notice it was always *our difficulties* and not the *difficulties I have caused by leaving you all for someone else.* It always riled me back then and it still does today. My wife hated the language that I used to describe our split. I referred to her as "leaving me for another man", which to my logical mind was precisely what had happened. One day she was living with me, the next day she was living with him. A simple fact. What was complicated or controversial about that?

She preferred to talk about our 'separating' and that her living with someone else was a consequence of the separation. I just wanted her to apologise for the pain and damage she had caused by the brutal way in which she had left us. It has never happened—although she did recognise that our break-up going on at the same time as my father's death was "not ideal timing". The mistress of understatement, my wife. No doubt if we had been living in Europe at the time of the outbreak of bubonic plague, she would have told me to be careful when I went out as there was "a bit of a sniffle going round".

Anyway I digress, back to the Christmas conversation, my wife was talking again.

"I've been thinking that, as the girls live with you and I don't see much of them, I'd like to take them to Brisbane with me for Christmas. My parents miss the girls and want to make sure they are all right. It will be good for them. After all, you took them to England in September so it is my turn to have them for these holidays."

What? What about me? I had done the hard yards for the last few months and was looking forward to some time with the girls when they were off school and I was off work. And did she think that I would be happy about being on my own at Christmas? Was this a bit of a power play—take the girls to see her family in an attempt to convince them that she and the girls had a good relationship and that they were happy to be with her?

"Have you talked to the girls about this?" I asked.

"Not yet. I wanted to talk to you about it first. I thought you might like to go back to England for Christmas this year. You've never been back at Christmas and, as this is the first year your dad won't be there, it makes sense for you to be with the rest of your family."

Credit where credit is due—she knew me well.

"If I go back to England I would want to take the girls with me," I replied.

"No way. I've hardly seen them for months and I'm not having Christmas without them." She was starting to get angry.

"Well I don't want to have Christmas without them either. So I don't want them to go to Brisbane."

We were good at this. We hardly agreed on anything, so this conversation came quite easily. It was hang up time. Nothing more to say. Nothing achieved. But it didn't go away. A few weeks later there was another Christmas conversation.

17 Happy Xmas (war is over)

"As Christmas is a family time I think it would be nice if we spent some of it together," was my wife's opening gambit. "Perhaps we could have lunch together in the house? We could even buy joint presents for the girls. It would help them to understand we still get on and that we are still part of a family."

I had stopped listening. Was this some form of cruel joke? What sort of message would this send to the children? This wasn't an amicable split. I was still angry and hurting. The simple fact was that we didn't get on, so why try and pretend that we did? And we weren't still a family. Our family times were now all in the past. And besides, what would we talk about around the lunch table? How well her new life was going? The lovely present her soul mate had given her for Christmas? The fact that I was a lonely man who slept wearing oven gloves in a forlorn attempt to prevent myself from going prematurely blind?

But I had to start listening again; she was still talking.

"I've been thinking more about Brisbane. I would still like to take the girls there over Christmas. I understand it wouldn't be fair to take them away on Christmas Day so I would like to take them the day after Boxing Day. We will be gone for ten days. I've told the girls and they are excited about it. My family haven't seen Sophie and Annabel for a while and it's not fair that they should suffer as a result of our difficulties."

That phrase again. *Our difficulties.* Did I get a say in this?

"I'll speak to the girls and get back to you," I said, ending the conversation.

I was disappointed. I had worked hard over the last months to get our lives back on some kind of track. I had to take the period between Christmas and New Year as leave and I had been looking forward to spending it with my daughters. And of course, part of me wanted to wreck my wife's plans.

The girls and I sat down together and we discussed Christmas in a very mature and sensible way. They told me they were under a lot of pressure from their mother to spend more time with her. They weren't yet ready to do this and were resisting the pressure, but they were finding it hard and emotionally draining to keep saying no. It wasn't a position that children should be placed in. They were looking to me to help them find a compromise.

I was also a bit cynical about my wife's motives. It turned out her soul mate would be having Christmas lunch with his wife and daughters and was then going away on holiday on his own. So my wife would be at a loose end and she needed some company. All these mind games and subterfuge. Shouldn't it just be about the children?

I got back to my wife. I told her she was welcome to come over for a drink on Christmas morning but that the girls and I would prefer to have lunch by ourselves. I also shot down the joint present idea. My wife had happily offered to go out and buy the joint presents. I knew what that would likely mean—she would get all of the credit for buying great gifts and I would end up with a big bill. No thanks—we were no longer a team—I was quite capable of buying my own presents.

I relented on the trip to Brisbane. The girls didn't really want to go, but they recognised how important it would be for their mother and that they had to compromise in some areas. I felt proud of them—and, rather self-righteously, put it down to the quality of my parenting.

There was a further tweak to the plans. My wife would collect the girls on Christmas morning and take them round to her house for breakfast and presents. She would then bring them back home and have a drink with me, while the girls opened their presents from my side of the family. The girls were happy

17 Happy Xmas (war is over)

with this plan on the basis that the soul mate, who they still hadn't met, wouldn't be at my wife's house. They didn't want to spend any part of Christmas with him.

It proved to be a bizarre Christmas morning. My wife arrived early dressed up in her finery; the girls appeared from their bedrooms dressed down in their pyjamas. I don't know whether they couldn't be bothered to get dressed so early or whether this was a form of protest against the plan. Anyway, off they went with my wife.

This now left me at a bit of a loose end. It was Christmas morning and I was on my own. I don't mind being on my own sometimes but on this day I was very unhappy about it. This was not the type of Christmas I was used to; I was used to the house being full of noise and excitement, not silence. I half thought about playing my Frank Sinatra Christmas carols CD and hitting the champagne, but decided to take the dogs for a walk instead. Merry Christmas to me!

I loaded the dogs into the car which made the day feel like a typical Saturday morning. I expected, and wanted, the dog track to be deserted so that I could wallow in my self-pity and justify my belief that I had been hard done by. But to my surprise, quite a few other people were also out for Christmas morning walks and the dog track was fairly busy. I also noticed, rather sadly, that I was the only person walking solo. I received a few glances and muted greetings from my fellow canine lovers. Were they simply assuming that I was a fundamental Jew, with no friends, and that I was exercising my right to not celebrate Christmas? This musing about the Jewish faith brought back memories of my circumcision, not a particularly nice thought given that I had to wrap bacon around my chipolatas when I got home.

It was only a short walk and when I got back home I was

surprised to see my wife's car in the drive. Back already. I let the dogs in and shouted out that I needed to go to the loo. My bladder was fine, in reality I needed some time to compose myself before going into the lounge room and becoming part of a scene that should have been a familiar and happy one—my children opening presents on Christmas Day—but was now going to be truly awkward. As I walked into the lounge room, I experienced my second surprise of the day. My wife wasn't there.

"Where's Mum?" I asked the girls.

"She's gone," said Sophie, very matter of fact.

"Why?"

"I just said 'Bye Mum' and she left," Sophie continued, without a hint of emotion. "Now can we get on with Christmas please?"

That must have been hard for my wife and, for the first time since she had left, I actually felt a bit sorry for her—it being the season of goodwill and all that. It was also tough on Annabel. She had wanted there to be some harmony on Christmas Day and later complained to me that Sophie always ruined things.

To my further surprise, I called my wife. I felt that it was important to talk to her, although I didn't know what I was going to say—whether I was going to sympathise with her, apologise, or invite her back round. But it didn't matter. She was too emotional to talk. All I managed to hear her say was something about how upset and disappointed she was that her children had been so rude and uncaring towards her. Isn't there some phrase about reaping and sowing?

So the three of us got on with our Christmas. We opened some presents, I had a glass of champagne, I put the chicken on, the girls put Christmas bows on the dogs, I had another glass of champagne, the girls laid the table with our familiar

17 Happy Xmas (war is over)

Christmas decorations, I had another glass of champagne and we opened the rest of the presents.

Time for lunch. We pulled crackers, put on stupid hats, told jokes and laughed. Did it feel like Christmas—or was it just a slightly enhanced version of Sunday lunch? I'm not sure. It didn't feel right that it was just me, Sophie and Annabel, but it was all we had so we made the most of it. Meanwhile, I knew that my wife was having probably an even stranger Christmas; she had secured an invite to a friend's lunch as her soul mate was with his own family. A bizarre situation for three families but this is one of the realities of separation—life becomes very different and very difficult, and the concept of family gets completely distorted. If people could experience the reality of separation for six months, would as many marriages end up this way?

To try and make it seem more like a normal Christmas, I drank a bit too much and we decided to play Monopoly. My eldest hates it, my youngest loves it and for me it brings back memories of my own childhood Christmases. It was a long game. My youngest won, as she normally does, and she made her victory as sweet and as drawn out as possible by continually letting me off some of the rent that I had to pay to keep me in the game longer. Sophie had capitulated hours earlier by entering into a crazy property deal with Annabel which left her almost broke. Bankruptcy, and an early exit from the game, was then inevitable.

A couple of movies later and it was bedtime. The girls said how much they had enjoyed the day. I'm sure they felt that it had been as weird as I had and I couldn't believe that Christmas 2007 would make it anywhere near to the top of the list of best Christmases ever, but it was kind of them to at least pretend it had been a good one. They knew I was struggling, and they wanted to give me a boost.

We all went to bed early. I had agreed to take the girls to the Boxing Day sales in the morning, and we wanted to get there before the crowds.

18

Can't fight this feeling

Next morning we were up at eight o'clock. The girls were very excited; I was feeling a bit shabby as I had indulged in a few extra glasses of wine on Christmas evening. It was going to be a hard morning so I decided that a cooked breakfast was in order for everyone. Our target destination was Chadstone, the biggest shopping centre in the southern hemisphere. I was pretty confident it didn't open until ten o'clock so we were in no rush.

As we approached Chadstone I started to doubt my confidence in regard to the opening time. There were cars everywhere. There were even cars parked on nature strips. I hate Chadstone on a normal weekend—the car parks are my particular nightmare—but today it was insane. I drove through two car parks that were completely jammed with not a single space in sight, just a stream of cars going round and round and round. My Christmas spirit and feelings of goodwill to all men were fast disappearing. There was literally nowhere to park. It was hopeless, and the girls were getting tense as we were wasting valuable shopping time. In the end, I told them to jump out of the car and said that I would find somewhere to park and catch up with them later.

I drove back out of the shopping centre and eventually found a parking spot in a side street. I slumped in the car seat building up the courage and energy to actually go into Chadstone. I would happily have sat in the car for a couple of hours except it was a baking thirty-five degrees and I had a hangover. I had no choice. If I didn't go into Chadstone I would be struck down by a combination of heatstroke and extreme dehydration. It was literally a matter of life and death.

This was virgin territory for me. Normally my wife took the girls to the Boxing Day sales and she would be as excited as they were. This was no place for a man. I should have been at home having a beer and watching the cricket.

I suspected that it might be a little busy inside the shopping centre but I was wrong—it was absolute madness. The walkways were teeming, it was loud, there were queues just to get into some of the shops and women were trying on clothes where they stood, in full view of everyone else. It was a feeding frenzy of noise, greed and bargains—and I hated it.

I had no idea where to go. I sent Sophie a text—"Have you had enough yet?" The reply was not encouraging, they had only just started.

I desperately needed to escape the crowds and decided to try the familiar and comforting surroundings of David Jones. I hoped that it may be a more relaxed environment. Wrong again. The ground floor was as crowded as Amsterdam's red-light district when there's a two-for-one special going down. I pressed on and headed for the usual place that I hang out while I am waiting for the girls, the TV and electronics floor. But this was no better, today it was packed with geeky-looking blokes spending their Christmas vouchers on new RAM and routers.

My energy levels were alarmingly low and my Christmas Day over indulgence was beginning to take its toll. I needed coffee. So I fought my way out of David Jones and headed for the nearest coffee shop. It was completely full of course. I had to wait twenty minutes to get served and, because I was flying solo, I didn't have a wingman to nab a table as it became free while I preserved my position in the serving line. Eventually I had a coffee but nowhere to sit. I stood there surveying the chaotic scene. It was absolutely crap. Crap? That gave me an idea. Where was the one place I could guarantee somewhere to sit? The gentlemen's lavatory! I thought about my phobia of doing a No.2 in a public place. Today would have to be the day I kicked that phobia right out of the park. I 'borrowed' a newspaper from the coffee shop. The sign said that they were for patrons only—well, I was a patron, it was just that my seat was going to be in a different location.

Surprisingly the gents' loo was not too busy and, as an added bonus, the lavatorial sanitation engineer had just completed an inspection. I walked in with my coffee and newspaper and, taking a deep breath (which was probably a mistake given the environment), I chose the end cubicle. Disappointingly, it looked as though it had been recently used. I wiped the seat down and covered it in toilet paper so as to avoid the transfer of any germs or bottom warmth. Halfway through my wiping I realised that, as I wasn't going to be using the seat for its proscribed purpose, I was wasting my time. So I just put the lid down and sat on that instead.

And guess what? It actually wasn't too bad. In fact, it was a bit like a typical Sunday morning, sitting on the throne at home while reading the newspaper. Granted, I wouldn't normally involve a cup of coffee in this operation, but that was just a bonus. There was a bit of huffing and puffing from some of the other cubicles and the occasional waft of something nasty, but I found that I could tune the sounds out and, by pushing my nose deep into my coffee cup, I could eliminate any unsociable odours. All in all, it was quite calm and relaxing and much, much better than the frenzy of Chadstone itself.

Half an hour later I had finished my coffee and was bored of the newspaper. I also began to wonder whether anyone had noticed that the end cubicle was permanently occupied. Was I at risk of a paramedic breaking the door down after being tipped off that there might be an unwell person in the toilet? How would I explain my loitering in the cubicle? Was it illegal to occupy a toilet stall for this long? Would I be deemed to have stolen the newspaper? Would I be fined and thrown out of the shopping centre? I had a flashback of being carried out of the school classroom on my chair.

I started to get a little stressed. And worse, the combination of anxiety and coffee was beginning to work on my intestines. I needed to go. I had no choice. So I converted the toilet from a seat back to a toilet and, without thinking about it too much, I went. I wouldn't classify this as a miracle of 'water into wine' proportions but for me it was almost equally as impressive. I had exercised my democratic right to do a No.2 in a public place and I wasn't an emotional wreck. I had made a choice, conquered my fears, and I had come through.

I left the gents beaming from ear to ear. In hindsight it was not really a good look—given that I had occupied the cubicle for thirty minutes—but I couldn't help it. I had beaten a phobia that had been with me since childhood. This was a cause for joy and celebration worthy of Christmas itself. I wanted to shout to the rooftops and tell people about it—but I didn't want to get locked up on Boxing Day, so I made do with a permanent smile on my face and kept the event as my own special secret.

When I met up with the girls and their shopping bags to take them home they were surprised to see me so happy. They asked me what I had been doing and why I was smiling as, from their perspective, my lack of shopping bags meant that I had no reason to be happy. I simply told them I had found a fantastic new coffee shop and left it at that. But the truth was so much more. I had cured my No.2 phobia. I felt confident that when nature called I would be able to respond, wherever I happened to be. It was a magnificent, life-changing event.

And, despite a few hiccups and doubts over the last few years, I have found the mental and physical courage to deposit my lunch in a range of public places—with only one exception, early morning at the Qantas Club lounge at Melbourne airport. I still can't go there. There is always a queue for the sit down toilets, which means (a) there is no choice of stall, you need to go immediately into the 'next available', regardless of what has been left behind, and (b) people are waiting to take your spot so you are under extreme pressure to perform on a timely and efficient basis. The Qantas Club toilets are my own personal Everest and I doubt whether I will ever be able to conquer them.

The next morning, amazingly, it was the day after Boxing Day, or December 27th to be precise. A day I had been dreading. My wife picked the girls up at 10 o'clock and, in an instant, they were gone for their ten day trip to Brisbane. The front door closed and I felt totally alone—probably because I was, in fact, totally alone. The house was empty and completely quiet. It was so sudden. One minute the house was full of life and the next minute—nothing. I walked around for a while feeling a little dazed and then went and sat in each of the girls' bedrooms. I looked at the possessions, which they were so proud of, smiled at their photos and made their beds properly. It felt as though they had been taken away from me.

It was depressing. I imagined there were probably thousands of single fathers all over the world sitting in their houses, alone. For those without custody of their children this would be what they experienced every day, and it was awful. If Christmas Day had been difficult, then the rest of Christmas was not going to be much better.

I remembered the words of the counsellor who I had been to see when my wife left. He was a tough guy, looked like a former rugby league player, and was very much of the no nonsense, matter of fact genre of counsellor. His parting message to me was "Don't get depressed". Easier said than done, but I knew that I couldn't sit around for the next ten days feeling sorry for myself. The girls were gone and there was nothing I could do about it. They would be well looked after so I didn't need to worry about them, miss them by all means I told myself, but don't get down about it. After all, it was only ten days.

I resolved to take advantage of my enforced break from parenting and make the most of my free time. And that's what I did. Not in a go crazy, rock and roll kind of way; more in an old bloke on his own at home kind of way. I watched a lot of soccer, swam in the pool, walked around naked (I'm not sure why), did a bit of running, read some books and enjoyed the fact that every time I went into the kitchen it was exactly as I had left it. I only had to look after myself and for a while life was all about me. It was relaxing, and I hadn't realised how important and beneficial this time to recharge would be after the trauma and intensity of the previous six months. It's a good thing, when you are part of a married couple and your responsibilities are shared, to get a break from time to time. It's even more important when you are on your own. I knew then that, if I was to grow as a father and deliver on my commitments to my children, I would need to have a break from time to time.

At the end of the ten days I was really looking forward to having the girls back. I had enjoyed my 'time off' but the house was too big without them, I was missing them and starting to get a bit lonely. They returned in a ball of energy and excitement, bags dropped in the hallway, wanting to hear about what I had been up to (not much), telling me what they had been up to (a lot) and raiding the cupboard for snacks. The kitchen became an instant mess, but I loved it.

I had never had a reunion like this before, even during my days in England when I would often be away for a week or more due to work commitments. It touched my heart and my eyes welled up—again. Their coming home brought home to me how much they had missed me and how important I had become in their lives. I was at the centre of their world. I was touched, and reflected again that this was something I would never have experienced in my earlier, pre-separation life.

Annabel burst into the family room and, using a pen she thought was designed for use on glass, wrote "We Love Dad" over and over again across the windows. Unfortunately it was the wrong pen and her words had a semi-permanent look about them. My wife, who was still inside the house, advised me to rub it off as soon as possible. She was worried it would stain the windows and she believed that the house would be going on the market soon. Maybe there was a simpler explanation—sometimes the truth hurts.

19

Slide it in

During January, Alison and I began to see each other regularly, but not frequently. She had her children on a full-time basis, as their father was working in New Zealand, and I had mine on a full-time basis. Neither of us had a lot of free time and so we had to search out opportunities to spend time together—the occasional evening, or a weekend dog walk. The other complication was that neither of us wanted to tell our children about our emerging friendship at this point—we weren't 'going out', we were simply exploring the possibility of going out, and we didn't want to give our children anything unnecessary to worry about. My girls were still adapting to life without their mother and Alison's boys had not enjoyed her previous relationship and were glad that it was over.

We talked a lot and learned a lot about each other. We got on well. We had similar values, believed in putting family before self, had been through the trauma of separation and had recently come to the end of long term relationships. We liked each other. We laughed a lot and made each other happy.

Keeping our evolving relationship quiet from our children meant that it felt a bit like having an affair—except there was no sex involved. It was exciting to make arrangements to meet somewhere discrete for an hour or so before hurrying home. And because we had not had sex, or even kissed, there was also the excitement and anticipation that this would likely happen in the near future. It really was a bit like being a teenager again, except I didn't have acne or a semi-permanent erection. In reality the opportunity for sex was not going to arise very easily because we always met in public, although I assumed that it was only a matter of time before it did. But of course we never discussed the subject.

Then, in late January, Alison's boys went to New Zealand for ten days to visit their father. This meant that she was now on her own so finding the opportunity for us to be alone became 50 percent less difficult. One Saturday night I managed to arrange for both my girls to go to friends' houses with midnight pick-ups, thereby creating a window for Alison and I to indulge in a wider range of activities than our usual walking and talking, should we choose to take it.

I dropped the girls at their social events, picked up Alison, and we went out for dinner. It was a normal evening, but for a hint of tension and an undercurrent of possibility. We were a pair of Cinderellas knowing that we had until midnight before life would return to normal. Did I eat faster than normal? Maybe. Did Alison pass on dessert? Definitely. Having finished dinner in record time, we had to decide what to do and where to go next.

"What shall we do next?" Alison asked.

"I'm not sure," I replied. "What do you think?" Please don't suggest the cinema, I prayed.

"Would you like to come back to my place for a quick drink?" Alison suggested, as casually as if we had known each other for years.

"That would be nice," I replied, doing my best impression of Cliff Richard. Butter wouldn't melt in my mouth.

We drove to her house in silence. On arrival I walked

around her lounge room very shiftily, consumed by pre-match nerves. Again it reminded me of my teenage years and going round to a girlfriend's house during the day when her parents were out. Would we? Wouldn't we? How long did we have? What if her mum came back and caught us? I remembered that as a teenager a returning mother had caught me out one fateful afternoon. I was upstairs in her daughter's bedroom, desperately trying to 'progress the play' and move from second to third base. It was long, hard, slow work but I was being well rewarded for my patience and making good progress—until I heard a car pull up in the driveway.

A quick glance out of the window and we both rapidly snapped into recovery mode. I pulled my jeans and shirt on, no time for my undies, and rushed downstairs, sat in the lounge room and picked up the newspaper. My girlfriend had beaten me down the stairs and was already in the kitchen putting the kettle on (And why not? Even horny teenagers like a nice cup of tea in the middle of the afternoon). I heard her mum come in with the shopping. She walked into the lounge room.

"What have you two been up to?" she asked.

Was that a loaded question or was she just being polite? I felt myself going bright red as I looked up from my copy of the *Knutsford Advertiser*, which I realised might actually be upside down. It was truly awkward. I thought that, on this occasion, it might be better to avoid the truth, so I went for a distraction.

"Hello, Mrs Dixon," I squeaked and, referring to an article in the newspaper, added, "Apparently they are going to be digging up the High Street again."

"Hi Mum, I'm just making Mark a cup of tea," my girlfriend chirped from the kitchen.

She may as well have added that she was going to get my slippers and cardigan to complete the highly implausible image of an old, married couple. Her mum looked at us both, slightly cynically.

"Actually, I've just remembered—we need to go and meet Noel and Julia," my girlfriend continued. "I'll just go upstairs and get my jacket."

It was good of her to go and retrieve my undies, although it did mean that I had to find another item of local news in order to maintain my fragmented conversation with her mother.

We left the house, naively thinking we had got away with it, but also realising that we had nowhere to go. So we went to the fields at the back of the houses and, while the mother drank my now un-required cup of tea, no doubt thinking she had saved the day, I did her daughter behind a hedge. Two bases in one day—that was real progress.

And now, as a forty-five-year-old, I was alone in another girl's house and the same questions were going through my mind. Would we? Wouldn't we? Only this time I knew how much time we had, and I didn't think there was much likelihood of a surprise visit from her mum.

It was a warm night and we sat outside having a glass of wine. Alison was talking but I couldn't focus. I wasn't sure how to approach a physical exchange. Should I ask her permission, or tell her what I had in mind to get her thoughts? Not very romantic. Should I just make a move? But what if she wasn't ready for a bit of 'lovin' and rejected me? I was nervous. I hadn't been in this situation for some twenty years. I couldn't really remember what to do and I didn't know whether the rules for forty-somethings were different to those for twenty-somethings. Time for a well thought through and cunning plan—I decided to count to ten and then just go for it.

I stood up and stepped away from the chair. Alison looked a bit surprised.

19 Slide it in

"Are you off?" she asked, uncertainly.

Without speaking, I took a step towards her and leaned slightly forward. I was now looking at the top of her head and realised that, as a result of my rather clumsy manoeuvre, my crotch was positioned directly in her line of sight. She had stopped talking. I guess it's difficult to know what to say when your vision has been completely obscured by the top of a man's trousers. To get out of this tricky position I decided to kneel down. The concrete was a bit hard but at least we were now at the same height.

"Are you going to kiss me?" she asked.

I moved my head in closer. We both had our eyes open. I loomed over her like a dentist. We were far too close for comfort. Awkward. I had two choices—either retreat, or complete the move. So I closed my eyes and kissed her. A few seconds later I opened one eye to check on what was happening. Alison's eyes were closed which I took as a good sign. Unfortunately she then opened one eye, which made things awkward again. I quickly re-closed mine.

I was enjoying the kiss but I knew that I had to stop; my body was in too much pain. The metal arm of the chair was digging into my stomach, which wasn't too bad, but my knees were suffering. The pressure of the cold, hard concrete was causing them to ache and they were beginning to seize up. I was too old for this position. I broke off the kiss and slowly staggered to my feet, my knees were killing me and I was moving like an old man. God knows what Alison was thinking.

"Are you okay?" she asked, with some concern.

"Yes," I said, attempting to regain my composure. "I'm just a bit stiff."

"Oh."

I realised what I had said.

"Oh, no," I gabbled. "It's just my knees. Everything else is fine...I mean...I've been kneeling down and..."

"Shall we go inside?" She saved me.

"Good idea."

We sat on the sofa and talked for a little while. Then we started kissing again. It was a lot more comfortable. Thirty minutes later we were still kissing. This was weird. In my previous sex life thirty minutes was enough time to dispense with the opening formalities, deliver the main event and be back sat on the sofa watching the football highlights. This was uncharted territory. I hadn't spent so much time at first base since puberty. What were the rules? Should we keep going? Should we stop and leave the other bases for another time? It was all a bit confusing.

The same thoughts were clearly going through Alison's mind—except she was brave enough to suggest a next step.

"Would you like to move into the bedroom?" she asked me, a little shyly.

"Only if you think it's a good idea," I replied.

"I don't know. Do you think it's a good idea?"

"I do if you do."

"Okay then."

It was hardly the most romantic or passionate way forward. We sounded like a married couple deciding whether or not to change the tiles in the bathroom. Why didn't I just sweep her up in my arms and carry her into the bedroom like a real man? Probably because I would have put my back out, or slipped on the step leading down to the hallway. But I felt that I should at least have tried.

Alison asked me to give her a couple of minutes and disappeared into the bedroom, leaving me alone in the lounge room. I felt as though I was in the doctor's waiting room. I picked up a magazine from the coffee table, flicked through a few pages and put it back down again. I checked my watch. Eighty-seven seconds had passed. I waited a bit longer. After the allotted two minutes I moved to the bedroom door. I had two options. I could either burst in, undressing as I went, a passionate sex god armed and ready, or I could knock on the door to make sure that she was ready. Obviously I chose the latter approach.

"Are you ready?" I asked, rather lamely.

"You can come in now," I heard her reply.

It was almost pathetic, we were like two kids getting ready to play hide-and-seek, not two sexually experienced adults getting ready to play hide the sausage. I was nervous again. What if she didn't like my style?

When it came to the bedroom I believed, quite happily, that I was the sexual equivalent of the legendary Australian bowler Glenn McGrath. I was consistent, quietly effective and economical, with a good line and length and the ability to keep it nice and tight while nagging away at the off stump for over after over. I could tie an end down, as they say in cricket. But what if Alison preferred something a little more fiery and volatile than my metronomic approach allowed for? What if she was more of a Shaun Tait girl and liked it unpredictable and fast off the pitch; enjoying the uncertainty of someone who was erratic and would serve up some absolute rubbish from time to time, but who was also capable of delivering something sublime that was totally unplayable?

Anyway, too late to worry about that now, she was padded up and I was at the end of my bowling run. The umpire had called play. I opened the bedroom door. The room was dimly lit and Alison was on the bed. I joined her. We carried on where we had left off on the sofa, except this time our clothes were coming off. We were naked. It was an incredible feeling and totally different to what I was used to. She felt different to my wife, she smelt differently and she kissed me differently. I understood again why people had affairs. This was a massive high. It was exciting and I didn't know what was coming next.

But, of course, what was coming next was my Glenn McGrath impersonation. I was slightly disconcerted at first. The pitch was a bit different to the one that I was used to; it was like playing an away game after years of only playing at home. However, after a few alterations to my action, I found my game, and there I was metronomicly plugging away with what I thought was a pretty solid line and length. Alison seemed to be enjoying it and I felt my confidence begin to rise—I could do this after all. I threw in a slower delivery and a gentle leg break just to shake things up a bit, and then went back to nagging away at her off stump.

With my rhythm established, I decided to have a better look around the bedroom and take in the surroundings. There was a nice old wooden chest of drawers, a new chair and matching bedside tables. I also noticed that on one of the tables there was a photo of her two boys—and they seemed to be smiling directly at me. It was a lovely photo but I didn't need an audience and I was momentarily distracted by having them in my eye line while I was bumping away on their mother. I immediately averted my gaze but it was too late, I felt my line go slightly astray as I carelessly delivered a wide. Fortunately I recovered. I managed to shut the image out of my mind and regain my focus, I was soon back in the groove and my impeccable rhythm returned.

However, the thought of children had set me off on another track, and this one I couldn't ignore. Birth control. We weren't using condoms—and why worry about that, after all, grown-ups

19 Slide it in

don't carry STDs do they? But what about contraception? I simply assumed that, because Alison hadn't said anything, she was on the pill or used some other form of contraception. And maybe she simply assumed that, because I hadn't said anything either, I had, like a lot of men in my age group, been 'snipped'. I remembered Doctor Cock offering to perform a vasectomy at the same time as my circumcision; he was even able to offer a special price as he "would be down in that neck of the woods". I now regretted declining his offer but at the time I was too scared of having trauma to both my meat and my two veg, plus I didn't want to run the risk of coming round from the operation sounding like the next Robin Gibb. But, as a direct consequence of my fear, and now rather uncomfortably given the current situation, my pipes were in full working order.

I decided that I should say something before it was too late.

"Um, can I ask you something?"

Alison opened her eyes. "Sure."

I knew it would be difficult for her to have a conversation with me at this point. One of the downsides of my impeccable action is that I can't stop my head from bobbing backwards and forwards. It's unfortunate, but there is nothing I can do about it. I resemble a turkey walking at speed or a cat about to bring up a fur ball, except I don't make that horrible hocking sound, thank God.

I could see Alison was struggling to focus on my bobbing head while I was speaking.

"It's a bit embarrassing—but are you on the pill?" I asked, while maintaining my line and length as if nothing was wrong.

"No."

"Okay. It's just that my *vas deferens* haven't been severed."

"Sorry?"

Clearly the combination of my medically precise language

and bobbing head were making it difficult for Alison to understand what I was talking about.

"I'm still firing live rounds," I blurted. "We're having unprotected sex."

The emergency brake was applied. Alison stopped moving instantly.

"What should we do?" she whispered.

I couldn't reply immediately. Unfortunately my head had been in 'bob forward' mode at the moment the emergency brake had been applied, and I had suffered a mild whiplash injury as a result.

"I think I should withdraw," I suggested, as the stars flashed behind my eyes.

"That's a good idea," she agreed.

Very gently I removed myself from her. We were both careful not to make any sudden movements in case we set it off. It was as if we were disarming an unexploded bomb.

"Do you think it's okay?" she whispered again.

"I think so," I confirmed, as I carefully inspected my manhood for signs of leakage, although as the room was dark I couldn't be certain. I remembered the little old lady from my daughter's sex education session and her stark warnings about the risks of involuntarily spilling seed.

It wasn't a very romantic end to our first effort at making love. It was yet another in a long line of awkward moments. We both sheepishly got dressed, which was difficult for me. Getting my old fella back into my undies was as difficult as a small child trying to put a jack-in-a-box back in its—well, box. It kept bobbling around and springing out as if it was aware that its job wasn't yet finished.

We went back into the bright lights of the lounge room, both looking a bit dishevelled and feeling a bit embarrassed.

19 Slide it in

"Maybe I should go," I said.

"Okay," Alison replied.

We hugged and kissed at the front door. It was the first time that we had hugged each other in such an affectionate way and I desperately wanted to stay with her, but I had to leave to get the girls.

"I'll try and see you tomorrow," I said as I left.

I drove home. We had crossed the Rubicon and there was no going back. We were now going out and it was a good feeling.

Having uncorked the genie as it were, or at least almost uncorked it, there was no stopping our enthusiasm for finding opportunities to continue with our lovemaking. We were back to being a pair of teenagers looking for empty houses, only this time we were looking for opportunities when our children, rather than our parents, would be absent. Fortunately the scheduling gods were on our side and on Saturday afternoons the boys' basketball and the girls' dance overlapped, thus presenting the perfect opportunity for a quickie. For the first time in my life I actually looked forward to Saturday afternoon sport.

But once a week wasn't enough for these two lovebirds and in our desperation we became even more adventurous. We tried it outside in a park—unsuccessfully, due to fear of discovery by someone on a late night dog walk, or worse, a group of local boys or the community pervert. We even tried it in the back of my car—again unsuccessfully, due to the occasional sweep of headlights from a passing car and a general lack of flexibility on my part. I didn't seem to be able to get all my limbs and equipment in the right place at the right time.

We were struggling. We were too old for adventurous, outdoor sex. We needed to move back into the comfort of indoors and that meant one thing—we needed to tell the children.

20

Rock on

Alison and I both knew that we had to be very sensitive when we told our children about our blossoming relationship. Alison's boys had not had a good experience of another man being with their mother and, although my girls were more stable in their new lives, I felt it was a little early for another bombshell. The girls and I were getting to grips with our life as a family of three. I knew that they didn't want another adult in my life and, as a consequence, in their lives. They had seen the separated parents of their friends find new partners and, although I'm sure they knew that one day it would happen for me, I also knew that they hoped it wouldn't be until sometime down the track.

Alison and I decided that we would tell the children gradually, and also keep them one step behind the progress of our relationship. It meant making sure we were secure in each phase of our relationship before telling the children things had progressed. It wasn't completely honest, but we felt that it was the best approach in consideration of their feelings.

As an example, the first time that I wanted to bring Alison to my house when the girls were home, I told a white lie. Alison and I had been for our regular Sunday afternoon dog walk and decided that we didn't want to go back to our own houses at the end of it. We wanted to spend more time together—and have a nice cup of tea in fact.

As normal we had set out separately for our walk in our own cars. But on this occasion, rather than going home, Alison followed me to my house and parked around the corner. I went inside and found Annabel, Sophie was out with her friends.

"Hi Annabel. Do you remember Hayden from primary school? I just bumped into his mum when I was walking the dogs. I had a chat with her and thought I might invite her round for a cup of tea. Would that be all right?"

"Yeah, I don't mind," she replied. "That's fine."

"Do you know her?" I asked. I knew there was a chance she did, given that Annabel and Hayden had been in the same year at school.

"Um, not sure. Maybe."

"Okay. Well we'll just be outside."

It was simple. I don't know whether Annabel realised that I was being economical with the truth at the time—obviously she does now. Sorry Annabel.

Having been given the all clear, I sent Alison a text and a few minutes later she rang the doorbell. It was pretty easy, she and Annabel had a brief chat about nothing in particular and we then spent an hour or so sitting in the garden. Even the dogs got on well, my two were happy to welcome Tess, Alison's dog, into their back garden. The dogs celebrated having a friend over by each doing a little poo.

After Alison had gone, I went up to see Annabel in her bedroom. Again I played down the significance of my relationship with Alison. I told her that it felt weird having a woman round for a cup of tea but that I liked Alison and I might see her again. Annabel seemed completely unperturbed. I repeated the story with Sophie when she got home. Being that bit older, I think Sophie was suspicious that there was something more going on, but she said she was pleased for me.

The next step in the process was for me to meet Alison's boys. We chose a time when they were in the cricket nets adjoining one of our regular dog walking tracks. Alison had warned them she was going for a walk with me and that, if we saw them, I would come over and say hello. And that's pretty much what happened. It perhaps didn't go quite as smoothly as Alison meeting my girls. My 'children small talk' was nowhere near as polished as hers and the boys were a little shy. We had a brief chat, most of which they spent looking at the ground, but when I said goodbye they both took off a cricket glove and shook my hand. It was a good moment and I felt as though I had taken the first step, albeit a very small one.

As we turned to continue our dog walk, Hayden plucked up the courage to ask me a question.

"Who's your favourite cricketer?" he called out.

My mind froze. I had an image and I couldn't clear it. Out it came. "Glenn McGrath," I stated, confidently.

"He's good. My mum likes him too," Hayden replied. "But her favourite is Shaun Tait."

"Is that because he's from South Australia?" I asked, hopefully.

"Not really. She says that McGrath is a bit too dull and predictable and she prefers Tait because he's more exciting and he makes things happen."

I had nothing else to say. We continued with the dog walk.

It was two steps forward. Over the next month the girls got used to me having Alison around for the odd cup of tea and the boys got used to me dropping into their home. Alison and I pretended that we were just starting to get to know each other, when of course we were actually getting to know each other quite well, and on a completely different basis when the children weren't home.

The girls and the boys had different reactions to the new person in their parents' lives and we needed to treat them differently. The girls were more reserved and circumspect—particularly Sophie. She had been hardest hit by my wife's leaving and, partly due to her personality and partly because she was the oldest, had become quite protective of me. She had also taken on a little piece of the 'woman of the house' role. So it was only natural that she was more wary of Alison, and needed Alison to prove herself.

At the dinner table I casually told the girls I had seen Alison again and that I really liked her. I was hoping they would tell me that they thought she was absolutely fabulous and that they hoped we would get together. They didn't, of course, but they did agree that she was 'lovely'.

Eventually, when I felt the time was right, I told the girls that I was going to ask Alison to go out with me (even though we were already going out). I wanted their blessing. I wasn't sure what I would have done if they'd said they were unhappy about it. My life with the girls had been mostly about them, it was now time for it to be about me as well.

Fortunately the girls were pleased that Alison and I were a couple, and so we decided to make some ground rules about how this new relationship would work. The girls were happy for Alison to come over in the evenings but they weren't comfortable with sleepovers. They felt it would be too awkward for them. I understood this. It was their house too and I wanted to respect their feelings. I also had high hopes for my relationship with Alison and wanted to have the girls onside from the beginning. It was too important not to. I didn't want to go crashing headlong into this relationship without considering the children's feelings. One step at a time was fine by me. We weren't in a rush.

The boys were less complicated. I think their main concern was not that I would try and take over their house and lives, but that I would be a prick. I wouldn't win them over through conversation and making peanut slice as Alison had done with my girls. I needed to be fun—and that meant doing boy things. I engaged in ferocious discussions on the merits of *Medal of Honour* versus *Call of Duty*, including the differences between the PC and PlayStation versions. I used my knowledge of English Premier League soccer to help them update their FIFA '08 team lists for player transfers. It was fun; they had much better toys than I did when I was a kid.

But the clincher was a masterstroke—I turned up one Saturday afternoon with my electric guitar, an instrument capable of being both a thing of beauty and a source of mind numbing noise. So much so that you can have a lot of fun just by playing a single note, and this was the course the boys took as they indulged in their rock 'n' roll fantasies. It was painful. To ease this acoustic onslaught I hoped that, as they could cope with one note they might be able to cope with four, and I showed them how to play the riff from *Smoke on the Water*. Why not, it has been bastardised by hundreds of teenage boys over the last thirty-five years so a little bit more couldn't hurt.

I kept it simple and played it on the bottom E string for those of you of a musical persuasion. The results were outstanding. I instantly took on a god-like persona. Even Alison seemed impressed by my ability to create genuine, heart-rending, emotion from the old riff. It took the boys about thirty minutes, and what seemed like hundreds of attempts, to get it right. They would miss the top note, get the rhythm wrong or forget the finger position. I showed them again and again. But eventually they had it. They played it nonstop for hours, experimenting with the effects on the amplifier and the volume. Instead of being one note of pain it was now four notes of pain. But it was worth it, I was now fully accepted as one of the boys.

In hindsight, I think I made the mistake of trying too hard to be one of the boys and being too friendly, or at least too much of a peer, with Alison's sons. There would be times in the future when I would need to dispense some control and discipline over them, and this would be more difficult because of my overly matey start. Alison did better than me in this regard. Her relationship with my girls was more one of an aunt; she was able to provide a good combination of love, friendship, support and, when required, firmness.

In the eyes of our children we were now officially a couple and we moved our relationship forward quite quickly. Again, the boys were much easier than the girls. They had no problems with me staying over on the odd occasion when both my girls had a Friday or Saturday night sleepover to go to. Riley, who was ten, would even make me a cup of tea in the morning and sometimes hop into bed with us.

But eventually my girls were also ready to move things forward.

"Annabel and I have been thinking about a few things and it's now fine if Alison stays over some nights," Sophie announced one day, very solemnly.

It was clearly a big thing for them and I loved them for it, because they had taken the time to think about something that would be good for me, even though it might be a bit uncomfortable for them.

"Thank you," I said. "I appreciate you thinking about this, and thinking about what I would like."

It felt like complete role reversal and I could imagine having the same conversation with Sophie in a few years time, talking about whether I would be happy for a boyfriend of hers to have a sleepover. Would I be so accommodating when the boot was on the other foot?

"She will probably only stay the odd weekend night if her boys are both out," I told her, hoping she wouldn't feel that her house was going to be invaded. "Thanks again Sophie, I do appreciate it."

"That's okay Dad. Just keep the noise down. Don't forget that Annabel and I live here as well."

21

Relight my fire

Two months down the track my relationship with Alison was getting better and better. It was exciting and fresh. And as a result, I did things for her that I would never even have considered doing when I was living with my wife.

One hot Saturday night Alison came over for dinner. She was bringing some prawns and my job was to knock-up a salad. I decided that we would eat outside and set up every single one of my candles around the table and at other appropriately charming spots in the garden. Annabel was a bit confused about my new found enthusiasm for natural light, so I told her that they were citronella candles to keep the mosquitoes away. She seemed a bit sceptical, rightly so.

No matter, it looked great and it had the desired effect on Alison. She was impressed by my romantic streak. But was I really romantic? 'Romantic' would have been one of the last words my wife would have used to describe me—'practical', 'reliable', or 'tight-arsed' were probably the first words that would have come into her head. I'm pretty sure romantic wouldn't have made the list.

Was this just enthusiasm for a new relationship or was I, indeed, a latent romantic? And if I was would it last, or would it eventually disappear in the bin labelled 'apathy'? If I had created candlelit dinners for my wife would our relationship have survived? Did she go looking for romance because I wasn't providing any? Difficult questions, because the answers could indicate that I played a role in the collapse of my marriage—and I preferred to take the view that its failure was all my wife's fault.

It was a great evening. It stayed warm and we sat in the garden until the early hours. I played my favourite music, we drank good wine and we talked about what we wanted to do with the rest of our lives. I looked into Alison's big, brown eyes and knew that if I wasn't in love with her at that moment, I was getting very close.

One thing I did recognise was that, if I wanted my budding relationship with Alison to thrive, I would need to change my traditional approach to matters of the heart. Or at least maintain my current approach of going the extra mile. Relationships are hard work and, unfortunately, can easily get bogged down in the day-to-day drudgery of life. I resolved to keep my relationship with Alison vibrant. That meant more dinners like this, regular weekends away and occasionally jumping in the bath together on a cold Saturday afternoon.

All the things I realised, rather guiltily, that my wife had suggested we do more of and which I had dismissed as being unnecessary. I had got lazy in my marriage. I had taken my wife for granted. And at the time it didn't seem to matter. We had been together for so long and our lives were so intertwined—we had children together, an extended family, our house and mortgage. We were stable. We relied on, and needed, each other. Why did we need romance on top of all that? What was the worst that could happen—after all it wasn't as if she would leave me...

This last thought brought me back down to earth. I wouldn't get lazy with Alison. I knew that if I did it could all end very quickly and easily. Alison and I had nothing to tie us together. We didn't have children together, we had no extended family, we were financially independent of each other and we lived separately. We were together simply because we wanted to be together and because we were good for each other. We supported each other and made each other happy. Our relationship was largely above the drudgery of life and my romantic candles were all part of it. If we ever lost those feelings, did we have enough other 'stuff' to keep us together? And anyway, would we want to stay together without those feelings? I couldn't be complacent, I would need to work hard on keeping it fresh, and that was a good thing. And besides, Alison's reaction to my romantic efforts was fantastic. She loved it, and that inspired me to do more.

Romantic musings aside, I had two important and personal events coming up in my life and they both fell into the category of 'having more fun'. They were big deals and I wondered whether I should involve Alison in them at such an early point in our relationship. One was a Whitesnake concert and the other was my brother's 40th birthday party in the UK.

Firstly, Whitesnake. They were my favourite band when I was growing up. Formed from the remnants of Deep Purple, the vocalist David Coverdale had created a soulful, blues-based rock group. Forget the poodle-permed, US-style mid-eighties version of Whitesnake, they started out as a genuine English band. As I moved through my late teens, Mr. Coverdale had taught me everything that I needed to know about life. He was particularly insightful on the ups and downs of love, and the joy and pain that women can cause a young lad.

Dave told me what it was like to be "born to walk alone", introduced me to the joys of "skinny little girls in tight ass jeans" and encouraged me to be a "love hunter". If things got rough his advice was to do my "crying in the rain" and to learn to "carry my load down the long winding road". It was a complete all-round education, a perfect complement to my more formal school and university studies, and I was very grateful for it. Although, when I look back, there was never anything along the lines of "shag like you're Glenn McGrath", so I don't quite know where that aspect of my lovin' came from.

I had been to see the 'Snakes' every year from 1978 to 1983 before they lost their way a little and I grew up. But now they were back and heading to Melbourne. I had to go; it would be a pilgrimage of sorts. But should I take Alison? She liked her rock music but would watching a fifty-something Englishman, with the hair of a thirty-year-old and unnaturally white teeth, singing songs about love in all its varied forms mean as much to her as it would to me? And, if she witnessed me groaning along, eyes closed, imaginary lighter in my hand, during the emotional audience participation part of *Ain't No Love in the Heart of the City*, would our fledgling love affair be over?

I decided it was all way too personal. She wouldn't be able to come. As every man knows some things are better done alone, and this was one of them.

But my brother's birthday party was completely different. This would be a chance for us to spend some uninterrupted time with each other, with the added bonus of being able to sleep together for more than just one night at a time. I also wanted to show Alison off to my UK family, partly because I was proud of her and partly because it would show them that I was firmly on the road to recovery.

Given that we had only known each other for a few months, Alison was amazed when I asked her to join me on the trip. She had never been to England before, which made it even more exciting for her and also for me. In another display of my new found romantic side, I decided to add on a quick side trip to Paris, after all, what could be better for a pair of youngish lovers than Paris in the springtime?

The only thing holding us back was making arrangements for the children. This proved to be a lot easier than we expected. My wife agreed to move back into my house for the two weeks that we would be away, she was happy to spend time with the girls, and I was prepared for the likely loss of a few household items as a consequence. Alison's situation was a little more difficult, but fortunately her former husband would be on a trip back from New Zealand as part of his future relocation to Melbourne, and he was able to help out.

We were all set to go. We would stay a few days with my mum in Winchester, spend three days in Paris, come back to London on the train, stay with my brother, go to his birthday party and then head back to Australia. It would be busy but exciting and, most importantly, fun.

When I booked the flights I was pleased to get the two seats in the back row of the Qantas 747. These seats are right next to the rear loo but, on the positive side, it meant that we wouldn't have anybody else sitting next to us for the whole trip. As we didn't spend much time together, I thought a little bit of privacy would be a good start to our holiday. It wasn't quite as private as I had hoped. There seemed to be a permanent queue for the loo that started right next to our seats; the constant, semi-atomic sound of the toilet flush; and the occasional waft of pungent smells. Who thought that serving spicy fish stew to three hundred people in a slim metal tube would be a good idea? When I slept, the lavatorial environment caused my fevered dreams to be peppered with demons and 'difficult' toileting situations.

As always it was a long flight, but it was a nice to have a

travelling companion, especially one without the tendency to throw up every half an hour. Although, as it happened, I did get to see the inside of Alison's stomach during our time away, but fortunately not on the flight.

We arrived on a cold, but sunny, day in London and were picked up from the airport by my sister, who took us back to her house. It was great to be back and wonderful to witness Alison and my sister chatting away like a pair of long lost friends. Even better, Alison immediately won over my sister's children and, as our trip progressed, went on to have the same effect on the rest of my family. I couldn't help thinking how much my dad would have loved her.

We spent our first night in England at my mum's house. I told my mum that Alison would sleep in the guest room and that I would take one of the other bedrooms. I don't know why I did this. We had been looking forward to sleeping together, anticipating that the nocturnal element of the trip would be one of the highlights—the equivalent of a Test Series for my Glenn McGrath alter ego, rather than the 'one dayers' I had become used to. I suppose I didn't want to embarrass my mum or put her under pressure to make a decision as to where we should sleep. I went through with the charade of putting Alison's bag in the guest room and my own bag in the room with the two single beds that my daughters used whenever we stayed with Mum and Dad. I even went as far as giving both my mum and Alison a goodnight kiss when we went to bed.

But as soon as it was lights out time, Glenn left the pavilion and strode purposefully across the pitch, polishing his balls as he walked (or crept quietly along the landing to the guest room, to be more precise) and I snuggled in with Alison. I seem to recall taking a five-wicket haul that night.

We were acting like teenagers again. I knew that with our

jet lag we would wake up way before my mum did. What could possibly go wrong? And nothing did, we spent the night together and in the morning we were up and about before my mum came down for breakfast.

The next evening, emboldened by the success of the first night, I repeated the trick. I said goodnight as innocently as John-Boy Walton, waited for ten minutes, and then crept along the landing under the cover of darkness. I was sure there was a Whitesnake song that covered this aspect of life, *Still of the Night* or *Here I Go Again* maybe. We had to be up early the following day so, unfortunately, I only managed to get a couple of overs in before the umpire declared "bad light". We were leaving at five o'clock in the morning to make the short trip to Southampton airport to catch the flight to Paris. My mum had kindly agreed to drive us to the airport. I told her we would be getting up at 4.30am and that I would wake her up fifteen minutes later.

The next morning I was lying in bed at 4.25am re-living an unfortunate dropped catch off my nocturnal bowling and thinking about getting up. The guest room is next to my mum's bedroom and, as I lay there, I heard, to my horror, the sound of her bedside tea-maker kicking into life. I'm not sure whether these things exist in Australia or whether they are a peculiarly English invention but in a nutshell a tea-maker is a teapot with a timer. It's a simple concept. Before going to bed you program it to boil some water which percolates through the tea leaves so, when you wake up, there's a nice cup of tea waiting for you. You don't even have to get out of bed. It's a brilliant invention—a sort of combination of alarm clock and *au pair*. But right at that moment, I was cursing it.

I panicked. The only piece of clothing that I had in the guest room was my undies. Would my mum be having a cup of tea before she got up? Would I have enough time to creep back down the landing to the other bedroom? Would I get halfway down the landing before being caught in the spotlight as my mum came out of her room and turned on the hallway light? And why was my mum getting up earlier than our agreed time anyway?

I hesitated; I wasn't sure what to do. And the hesitation proved fatal. I was still lying in bed when I heard the door of my mum's bedroom open. Bollocks. I heard her walk down the landing to the other bedroom where she assumed I would be. Double bollocks.

"Mark, it's time to get up." I heard her call out softly. And then, because there was no answer, call out again. "Mark, it's 4.30, time to get up."

There was a pause while I imagined she looked into the bedroom to discover that I wasn't there. Meanwhile, I was holding the sheets of the wrong bed around me, paralysed like the proverbial rabbit in headlights.

I heard her footsteps come back down the landing and then she knocked softly on the door of the guest bedroom.

"Mark, it's 4.30, time to get up."

"Morning Mum, we've been up for ages—bloody jet lag," I chirped, as cheerily as I could, given it was so early in the morning. "I'm just helping Alison to pack. See you in a minute."

I doubted whether I had got away with it. Mind you, it had taken twenty-five years for my mum to finally spring me with a girl, and I had escaped some close shaves in my youth so, all in all, it wasn't too bad. Alison, of course, was terribly embarrassed. It taught us right for not being honest in the first place. We needed to stop acting like a pair of teenagers. Mum drove us to the airport and nothing else was said.

22

Love to keep you warm

A few hours later we were in Paris. It was cold and grey and not nearly as romantic as I had hoped. Still, we were staying in a boutique hotel and would be on our own for the first time, no children or dogs to worry about, no chores to do—it would just be the two of us. We made our way to the hotel. It was small. We were shown to our room. That was small too, in a cute European way. Basically a room just about big enough to accommodate a bed and a tiny ensuite with a sliding door, no window and, I also suspected, no extractor fan.

I felt a gnawing in the pit of my stomach. How was I going to cope with this? I thought about the combination of rich French food and a small ensuite with no window or extractor fan, and shuddered. It was probably all going to end in tears—literally. I hardly knew Alison. I was pretty sure I wouldn't be able to do my business so overtly and in such close proximity to her. I thought back to that horrendous day at school when I'd tried to fight my swelling intestines and hold out until home time, only for my efforts to end in glorious failure. And now, as an adult, did I have the physical and mental strength to hold on for three days and two nights until we were back in Blighty? I could only try. Ironically, although I didn't know it at the time, Alison was suffering from exactly the same fears.

I banished these thoughts and we strode off into the cold of

Paris. We did a lot of walking, a lot of sitting in cafes and a lot of talking. I was very happy. I knew Paris reasonably well and it was a pleasure to show Alison my favourite places and to discover new places together. We finished a fantastic day with a fantastic meal in a classic Paris bistro.

Next morning the sun was out and, through the tiny slit in the bedroom wall that masqueraded as a window, the city looked its best.

There was just one thing bothering me while we sat in bed having our early morning cup of tea. I had a No.2 that needed to be delivered, and it was keen. As I drank my tea, I studied the wall dividing the bedroom from the ensuite. It looked paper-thin. Was there any chance it could withstand the nuclear-like delivery brewing in my intestines? I doubted it.

I told Alison that I needed to do a wee and got out of bed. Once I was inside the ensuite I studied it again. It wasn't really a room as such; it was little more than a piece of cardboard wall hiding the bathroom from the bedroom. It was tiny and airless. I briefly wondered whether running the shower would provide me with sufficient cover—but it all seemed far too risky. I realised with a rising sense of panic that I would need to find an alternative delivery site. And then I had a brilliant idea.

"Why don't I go out and find us some fresh croissants?" I suggested, all bright and breezy.

"Oh, I thought we were going out for breakfast? Didn't you say you would take me to that special cafe overlooking the river?" Alison looked a bit disappointed.

Bugger. I had. But I had more pressing matters to deal with.

"Yeah, I did. But I've had a look at the map and I think it's a bit far. I'll buy some croissants from the bakery across the street and then we can go for a walk and get a coffee."

"Sounds good. How long will you be?"

"Not long. Ten minutes I hope." I couldn't be much longer; my body wouldn't allow me much more time. I got dressed, left the room and rushed down the stairs. I was a man on a mission. I had heard a lot of unpleasant stories about the free community loos in Paris, so this was going to be the ultimate test of my ability to deliver in public. Perhaps, because it was early in the morning, they had just been cleaned and I would have first-user advantage. That wouldn't be too bad. Then again, because it was early in the morning, maybe they were yet to be cleaned and were still carrying the detritus of a hard day and night's work. Probably the more likely scenario, I concluded.

I strode grim-faced yet purposefully across the small hotel lobby, concentrated on keeping an appropriate level of tension across my buttocks, and wished the smiling receptionist a tense *bonjour* through gritted teeth. I had no idea where the nearest public loo was but I was far too embarrassed to ask the twinkly-eyed, and slightly effeminate, receptionist.

But hang on. What was that? Could it be? It was! In the corner of the lobby there was a toilette. Oh joy! Oh rapture! And the even better news was that it was likely to be clean. I stopped in my tracks, scratched my chin as if deep in thought and then, as casually as I could but with a thumping heart, made my way towards the sanctuary of the toilette. I wanted the receptionist to assume that I was going out for a quick walk and, just to be on the safe side, had decided to stop for a quick tinkle before leaving.

I stood outside the door of the toilette and savoured my relief. I turned the handle and nothing happened. I tried it again. The door of the bloody thing was locked. I was momentarily confused. Was there someone else in there? Please don't tell me I would have to use a newly vacated toilet. And how long were they going to be?

I stood staring at the door in a semi-trance until a gentle tweak in my guts and a polite cough from the receptionist brought me back to my senses.

"Would *Monsieur* like to borrow the key to the lavatory?" the receptionist suggested, very gently and politely.

"Yes, thank you. That would be nice," I replied, trying to appear relaxed, as though he had simply offered me a second cup of coffee.

The receptionist held up a little key on a small dangly chain and gave it a shake.

"*Voila!*" he exclaimed, rather unnecessarily I thought. But there it was, quite literally the key to my salvation. I wanted it so bad.

I took the key and opened the door to a small, clean toilet—with a window. I opened the window out of respect for the next visitor to this little piece of heaven. It was glorious. Job done, I returned the key to the receptionist. I hoped I hadn't been too long.

"*Merci,*" he twinkled, holding out his hand to reclaim the keys, head tilted and eyes sparkling.

"*Merci,*" I replied, and turned to go back up the stairs. Whoops! Wrong move. I turned round, went past the reception desk again, smiled politely to the receptionist and disappeared out onto the street.

"*Au revoir.* Have a nice day." I heard the receptionist trill. Sod off I thought to myself, a little bit uncharitably.

It was still quite chilly outside and I wasn't really dressed for it. A quick walk round the block and I was back in the hotel lobby.

"Ah, *Monsieur—bonjour*—nice to see you again." The receptionist gave me a comedy French welcome. He seemed to be enjoying our little game. I walked past him with a grin, avoided eye contact and ran up the stairs back to the sanctuary of the room.

I opened the door and was hit by the blast of a strong, sweet smell carried on a wind of warm air. I almost gagged.

"Whoa," I exclaimed, involuntarily. What in the name of all that is holy was that? Within the confines of the small room it was overwhelming.

Alison looked a little sheepish. "I spilt my perfume. Sorry if it's a bit smelly."

It was more than a bit smelly, it was completely overpowering. And, strangely, the smell became even stronger when I went into the ensuite. It was a hideous combination of sweet and sour, as they say on *MasterChef.* Had Alison taken the opportunity of my absence to use the facilities? Is that why she wanted to know how long I would be? And that was exactly what had happened. My disappearance had been the cue for Alison to embark on a frantic scramble to deliver her own evil monster and desperately attempt to cover her tracks before I returned.

"Did you get the croissants?" Alison called out from the bedroom. She had seen me come in empty handed.

"No. They didn't look very good," I replied. "I think we should go out for breakfast after all."

Jobs done, we were both able to relax and concentrate on the rest of the day. The sun was out and Paris took on a whole new life. It's a brilliant city in the sunshine. We spent most of our time wandering around hand in hand, sitting on benches, popping into cafes and enjoying the city.

Eventually, we found ourselves at the foot of the Eiffel Tower. I had been there a number of times but it was a first for Alison, and seeing it through her eyes made it seem special to me again. It was magical. I was with a wonderful woman in a wonderful city and I wanted to mark the occasion. I held Alison close, looked into her eyes, and whispered that I was in love with her. It didn't come out as smoothly as I would have liked but it was heartfelt and I truly meant it. And besides, we were in Paris. What could be better than telling someone you love them in the City of Love?

And to cap it all off, Alison told me that she felt the same.

(Note: I now understand that Venice, and not Paris, is in fact the City of Love. Paris is more correctly known as the City of Lovers. I appreciate this is a subtle difference but I wanted to mention it in case I had caused any confusion.)

23

London calling

Our time in Paris had come to an end and we boarded the Eurostar train, which would take us straight to the centre of London. My brother was going to meet us at St. Pancras station. I am very close to my brother—he's my best mate—and I hadn't seen him yet on this trip as he was in Moscow when we had first arrived. I was really looking forward to our reunion and for him to meet Alison.

Every time I see my brother, regardless of how many months or years have passed, we pick up from where we left off. It's as though no time has passed at all. It's always brilliant to see him and this time was even better, because my little brother was about to be forty.

The plans for the party sounded exciting. He had booked the function room on the top floor of a trendy bar in Soho. This was a great part of London and another first for Alison, which I was looking forward to sharing with her. I was also looking forward to catching up with old friends and family. It would be the first time I had seen most of these people since my separation and I wanted them to know that I was getting my life back on track.

My brother lives in Clapham so, on the night of the party, we took a quick cab ride into central London and went for something to eat before heading to the venue. It looked good. A cool guy on the decks and a South American theme complete with a 'Tequila Girl' whose only job was to dispense shots to the partygoers. Sadly she didn't last long, she embraced a 'one for you, one for me' philosophy and was last seen propped up in the corner of the room, tequila supplies exhausted.

My brother warned us that, although he had dropped a reasonable wad of cash behind the bar, he didn't think his generosity would be sufficient to fund an entire evening of drinking for the whole party so he recommended we adopt a 'go hard, go early' game plan. And that's exactly what we did. Alison, in particular, seemed to be getting into the spirit of things. Because it was still early in our relationship, and this was one of the first parties that we had been to together, I had no idea of her capacity for alcohol. Mind you, she was always banging on about being a country girl and so I simply assumed that meant she could down her own body weight in booze. She certainly seemed to like her gin-and-tonics.

The party was on. It was a goody. I was having a great time, as you always seem to do when you haven't seen people for ages. Alison was on fire and being with her was so natural. It felt as though we had been together forever and she had known my family and friends for years. I was very proud of her.

I smiled at Alison and she came over to me, put her arms around my neck, and told me that she could see three of everything. I suggested we sit down for a bit and she then told me that she felt a bit dizzy. I wasn't too concerned, probably just a combination of jet lag, adrenaline and drinking a bit too quickly. Having sat down for a while, Alison confirmed that she was fine and decided a toilet break was in order. The loos were on the top floor and she disappeared up the stairs, demonstrating a very effective comedy walk underpinned by a double-handed grip on the banister.

23 London calling

I was a bit worried about her, so I decided to wait in the corridor outside the function room until she came back. It would also give me the chance to cool off a little. Five minutes passed. Ten minutes passed. No sign of Alison. I was now officially worried, so I found my mum and asked her if she would mind checking the toilets to make sure Alison was all right. Five minutes later my mum returned to say that Alison wasn't there, she had even looked under the cubicle doors for signs of life—nothing.

My worry was now full-on concern. Where the hell could she be? All I could think of was that Alison had come out of the loos when I was looking for my mum, gone down the stairs, missed the function room, ended up in the main bar on the ground floor and was now confused and wondering where the party had gone. Or maybe she hadn't even noticed she was in a different place and was still partying.

My mum searched the party while I rushed down to the main bar. It was packed. I pushed through the crowd as best I could but no sign of Alison. I went out onto the street, there were people milling everywhere. Shit. This was actually quite serious. She had no phone, didn't know the name of the bar that we were in and didn't know my brother's address. If she was out on the street she would be badly lost and, given that she was obviously quite pissed, very vulnerable. How on earth was I going to find her? What if something happened to her?

I went back inside. My mum had checked the toilets again but no joy. I could only hope that Alison was somewhere in the building. Surely she was still in the loo? There was only one thing for it. I called in my sister for a commando-style sweep of the ladies' loo. My sister has three young children. She knows all about the strange places kids can find to hide.

When it came to a search and rescue effort I couldn't think of anyone better qualified.

My sister and Mum teamed up to perform the sweep and, sure enough, I soon received a message that Alison had been found alive, but not so well. So not so well, in fact, that she wouldn't be able to rejoin the party until she had regained her composure. This took a while. Apparently it was coming out of her top and bottom. When she did finally come down the stairs I recognised that the umpire had raised his finger and it was game over. I said my premature goodbyes to my brother and family, and took Alison down to the street to find a taxi. Her evening reminded me of an Ian Botham innings. It had opened with a series of glorious fours and sixes and the promise of history being made, but it was only a matter of time before a top edge went flying high into the air to be taken by the wicketkeeper—chance of glory gone.

There is no polite way of saying it. Alison was a mess. But it wasn't all bad as tonight would be a night of firsts for me. My first 'first' was to witness the 'vomit into the handbag' manoeuvre. Prior to this moment I hadn't appreciated the thought, versatility and practicality that have gone into the design of the modern handbag. It's a phenomenon—there is so much more to a handbag than just being a place for a lady to lose her car keys, mascara, tampons etc. Two things in particular struck me about this. One, when pulled close to the face, like an oxygen mask, a handbag fits very snugly across a gaping mouth while leaving the nose clear for breathing, thus enabling the smooth transfer of vomit from person to receptacle. And two, you can fit a lot of regurgitated food and drink into even a relatively small handbag. It's obviously a Tardis sort of arrangement.

Armed with her handbag, Alison produced a very neat

display of vomiting. The cab driver, whose nervous eyes I could see in the rear view mirror, was particularly appreciative of her technique. Not a single drop escaped. In fact, apart from a crusty ring of dried, orangey vomit around her lips and on her chin, you would never have known anything was wrong—apart from that and the heinous breath.

Having managed the cab ride successfully, we were faced with a new challenge. My brother lives on the top floor of a four-storey building. There is a steep and narrow staircase up to his flat and Alison seemed to be completely lacking the arm and leg co-ordination required to get up it. However, after a few aborted efforts, I found that, if I stood behind her and she lay back in my arms, her body adopted an angle of thirty degrees and her legs went up the stairs quite easily. Having successfully got her into my brother's flat, I warmed my hands up, undressed her—in a completely appropriate fashion—and put her to bed.

Unfortunately, Alison was now in a really bad way. Her eyes were spinning and she was mumbling things like "never felt this bad before", "don't know what's wrong", "tell my boys I love them" and lastly "don't let me die here". It was quite dramatic and my eyes were brimming with tears. It wasn't so much the emotion, although it was a poignant moment, it was more her breath. It was eroding my will to live. Fortunately, I travel with one of those birdflu masks much favoured by the Asian community. I put this on and, with the fetid smell partially eliminated, I was able to think more clearly.

The reality was that I hardly knew Alison. I had no idea whether she was suffering from a severe reaction to something, or was just pissed. But she was clearly very distressed and worried that she wouldn't live to see her boys again. It was disturbing. There was a good chance, of course, that she would sleep it off—but what if she didn't? I thought about it for a few minutes. I was responsible for her so I couldn't take any risks.

For my second 'first' of the evening, I did something I had often dreamt of but never experienced—I dialled 9-9-9 and called the emergency services. The operator confirmed that an ambulance would be with me in five to ten minutes and suggested that, if I was able to leave the "victim" unattended, it would be helpful if I could stand outside the house and wave it down. I thought "victim" was a bit over the top, but I was confident Alison wouldn't come to any harm in the space of a few minutes and I wanted to witness the full-on siren blaring, lights flashing arrival of the paramedics. So I straightened her nightie, to prevent any embarrassing fall out later, and headed down the stairs.

I didn't quite get the extreme ambulance arrival that I hoped for. No siren, just the flashing lights, and it was hardly travelling at speed. I waved it down. Two paramedics jumped out.

"Did you call an ambulance?" the first paramedic asked.

"Mess I mid," I mumbled.

"Are you alright sir?" The second paramedic looked a bit puzzled.

I realised I still had the bloody anti-bird flu mask on. I took it off.

"Yes. I'm fine. The victim is upstairs." I adopted their vernacular, although quickly realised that this, along with the mask, might lead to the assumption that I was the guilty party.

Shit. I hoped they didn't think I was a pervert of the Hannibal Lector variety and that the reason for Alison's demise was due to some gruesome failed experiment. They both looked at me a little oddly, and I think one of them shook his head slightly as they passed.

Once they were upstairs with the victim they took her

blood pressure and a couple of swabs. They asked Alison her name—and she got it right! Their machine indicated that her blood alcohol reading was not excessive, so she was either a lightweight when it came to drinking or there was something more seriously wrong.

"We're taking her to hospital," medic one declared.

Although this sounded quite scary for Alison, on the positive side it meant that I was going to go for a ride in an ambulance. They expertly moved the victim onto a stretcher—there was just a hint of nipple slip but otherwise the nightie held up well—and tucked her under a blanket. I couldn't help noticing that the paramedics were quite hot in that 'rugged but handsome' way, the classic *ER* or *Grey's Anatomy* look. She will be disappointed to have missed this, I thought.

It was a bit of a challenge getting Alison and the stretcher back down the narrow stairs but with a bit of huff and puff they made it, with only a couple of dents to the plasterboards.

Cargo loaded, I was invited to sit in the back of the ambulance with Alison. I was hoping we would tear through the streets—but this clearly wasn't as serious a case as I had imagined. Obviously I didn't want Alison to be in any life threatening danger, but it would have been nice, in a way, if her situation had merited the siren and a bit of speed. I half thought about calling out that she had stopped breathing, to see whether that would bring a bit more urgency to proceedings.

By the time we reached the hospital Alison was starting to feel a bit better. She had calmed down in the ambulance and her panic seemed to have left her. She had also regained some of her dignity and wanted to walk from the ambulance unaided—but no, once the paramedics have got you it's compulsory to stay on the stretcher so that you suffer the humiliation of being wheeled into casualty as a total pisshead.

I was pleasantly surprised by the hospital. For a National Health Service affair in the middle of Tooting in South London it was actually quite a nice place to be on a Saturday night. It was warm and friendly, and there was a little machine that dispensed hot chocolate—the perfect place to recover after a party and dramatic night out.

Alison was taken to a bed in a curtained-off cubicle, where she suffered the further humiliation of having to change into a hospital gown, and we began the long wait for a doctor. I could see that she was getting sober—and angry. She wanted to go home, or at least back to my brother's flat. She argued with the nurse who did her blood tests, she argued with the orderly who told her that the doctor would be an hour and she argued with me. The hospital staff were adamant she must stay—she had, after all, taken advantage of one of their ambulance crews who arguably had more important things to do. And I was happy to stay longer as I was enjoying my hot chocolate.

Eventually the doctor arrived, by which time Alison was fully recovered. He checked her eyes and reflexes and told her the blood tests were clear and that she was free to leave. However, before she could go, he insisted on giving her a little talking to about the dangers of alcohol and how binge drinking was bad for your health and could result in you getting into dangerous situations. It was beautiful. I sat in my chair in the corner, nodding in agreement with the doctor, and self-righteously added in the occasional "that's right" and "definitely" to accentuate some of the more important points. I didn't think he was quite as dramatic or as compelling as I had been when spelling out the dangers of excessive drinking to Sophie, but then again, Alison was nearly thirty years older.

I had been in text contact with my brother throughout the ordeal and, once we had the all clear from the doctor, he came to pick us up. He brought Alison some flowers, which I thought was a nice touch given the circumstances. Dawn was breaking as we left the hospital. Alison was now feeling completely foolish and angry with herself, and was worried she had ruined the party. Simon lamented that it was his birthday and yet it was me who got to ride in the ambulance.

Next morning, the family gathered for a recovery brunch and a party debrief. Alison spent most of the day in bed as she was still being sick, and besides, she hadn't really been at the party long enough to contribute to the debrief. Naturally, we took the opportunity of her absence to talk about her. We all agreed that she must have eaten something that had set off a spectacular adverse reaction—an undercooked prawn, for example. She was Australian after all, so it was inconceivable that she couldn't hold her drink. The tests had shown her alcohol level wasn't too high—food poisoning was therefore the only logical explanation.

I too chose to believe the "something that she ate" conclusion. She had definitely been in a bad way when I called the ambulance and it certainly seemed as though she was suffering from more than just a bit too much to drink. In hindsight, I'm not so sure. Just over a year later we travelled to Whyalla for her own brother's fortieth birthday party. And, amazingly, the same thing happened. Alison started to feel unwell and we had to leave the party early, albeit this time by car rather than by ambulance. On this occasion she managed to get back to her mum's house in one piece, before spending a good half an hour on her knees in the bathroom hurling into the toilet. She obviously hadn't heeded the kind London doctor's words of wisdom.

To be fair to Alison these unfortunate events proved to be isolated exceptions. She has subsequently got her drinking under control and hasn't been ill since—apart from on New Year's Eve some six months later.

24

I hear you knocking

We returned from our trip to Europe jet lagged but happy, and Alison and I quickly settled back into our normal routine—living with our children, running our houses and snatching time together at the weekend whenever we could. Over the next months life became more stable from one aspect—I was getting better at being a single dad—but the ongoing battles with my wife meant that, in other aspects, my life was becoming more difficult.

A number of factors were driving the spiralling separation stress levels. My wife and I were well into our financial settlement (a nightmare, but more of that later); I hadn't 'given up' on being a single parent—I'm sure my wife had assumed that I would throw in the towel after a few months and that the girls would end up living with her; and now I had Alison in my life. I suspect that, from my wife's perspective, my life was going just a little too well. I knew that she didn't want me to be unhappy—and, in fact, genuinely wished me happiness—but perhaps I was too happy. I had the children, I was living in our family home, I had Alison and I had been to Europe. Maybe my life was going better than hers? This wasn't the way that things had been expected to turn out. Clearly, I hadn't read the script. She told me that things "weren't fair" and that I was "being selfish". Why? Apparently, because I was only thinking of myself and not her. I let that one pass—wasn't an outbreak of selfishness how this whole thing started in the first place?

The girls, caught between feuding parents, were also feeling the stress and I could tell they needed a break. Fortunately, the perfect opportunity arose. Their dance school was going to be performing for a few days during the school holidays at the Gold Coast theme parks, so we decided to go up there a few days early and spend some time away from our daily lives. Alison, not wanting to miss out on a few days of sun after the Melbourne winter, decided that she would also come and bring her boys. This all sounds simple. But nothing is simple when you are dating a woman who also lives with her children full-time. Our short trip to the Gold Coast required logistics that the military would be proud of. Alison and the boys would act as the advanced party and head to the Gold Coast first, enabling them to spend some time together; I would follow with the girls a few days later and we would stay in a separate apartment but in the same complex; and a few more days later the girls would meet up with their dance school, the boys would fly back to Melbourne to spend some time with their father and Alison and I would spend a couple of days on our own. Simple really! And, just to make it a little more complicated, the girls were each bringing a dance friend with them and each friend would need to be collected from different flights at the Gold Coast airport.

The girls and I were travelling via Brisbane and so we decided to add in a quick pit stop via my wife's parents. Which was maybe a big and brave call on my part, but we were flying into their hometown and I had always got on well with them. Plus they had been very supportive of me. I knew it was the right thing to do and, despite everything that had happened, they were still the girls' grandparents—we couldn't pass through without saying hello.

We stayed with my in-laws for one night. It felt very weird to be in their house without my wife but everyone seemed reasonably relaxed. I'm sure my wife's parents were worried that I might go off on some rant about their daughter. And, in turn, I was a bit worried they might take me aside and give me a talking to about the fact that I wasn't being very cooperative with my wife and that the girls weren't seeing enough of their mother. But it was fine. We had normal conversations about what was happening in their lives and what was happening in our lives, and cleverly avoided referring to my wife at all. It was like a bunch of actors avoiding saying 'Macbeth'.

The only thing different was the sleeping arrangements. Normally, when we stayed there as a family, my wife and I would share her old room and the girls would sleep together in the study on a sofa bed. Tonight this would all change. Sophie was given my wife's room, Annabel had the sofa bed all to herself and I was relegated to a camp bed in the sleep-out, the old veranda. Was this to appease my in-laws, my wife's or my own sensibilities? I wouldn't really have minded sleeping in my wife's old room, but maybe she did. It was understandable but another reminder that, while things were the same at one level, they were very different at another. I was still part of the family but I was sleeping on my own, on the periphery of the house. I guess it reflected that I was now on the periphery of their family—more of a guest than a fully enrolled family member, even if this wasn't my in-laws' choice.

Our Gold Coast holiday was hard work but fun. The decision to have separate apartments was the right one, although it added significantly to the complexity and cost. Alison and I felt it would be hard for the boys and girls to be crammed into a single apartment together when they hardly knew each other, and that it might make things awkward for them. Again, we saw our relationship as a long-term thing. We were in no rush, we wanted to get it right, take things one step at a time and make things as easy as possible for the children—and, in hindsight, these were good decisions. So, in our multi-party holiday, we spent time as individual families, time together (mostly at mealtimes) and the girls spent time with their friends, as having a bit of independence was becoming more important to them. It worked well, and I was particularly pleased that the friends' parents were happy for their daughters to come with us. Vindication of my parenting and trust in me, I thought.

The only real downside was that Alison and I slept alone in our separate apartments. I had two of my daughters' friends with me and I didn't want to leave them on their own overnight, even though they wanted me to (!), and, similarly, it was not right for Alison to leave her boys. It was frustrating but, again, the right decision—and we had a few days on our own afterwards to look forward to, which would help to make up for it. My Glenn McGrath alter ego felt a bit snubbed at being dropped for a Test Match, but that just increased his desire to come out all guns blazing at the next one.

Unfortunately, because the financial settlement with my wife was in full bore at the time, I was nervous about leaving the house unprotected. I had never been too concerned about the majority of our possessions—they were mostly nice things, but ultimately only things—whereas my wife was able to describe every ornament and piece of furniture in our house, where it came from, whether it was a gift, how much it cost and so on. I was vague on these details, both in terms of what we had and what was valuable, although I was, of course, totally familiar with the model numbers and specifications of the TV, DVD player and HiFi.

But as the months since her leaving passed I had become

more aware of my 'things', and I also started to think that their number might be decreasing. It was nothing significant, just what appeared to be an incremental change. It reminded me of the time when, as a kid, I would horde and hide my Easter Eggs and then wonder whether my booty had decreased slightly when I had been at school (of course it had, my sister was taking one small piece a day). It was the same now. I would look at the mantelpiece and wonder, with a slightly nagging doubt that I might be imagining things, was an ornament there a few weeks ago? Similarly, didn't there used to be more pillows on the spare bed? I went to make a casserole and couldn't find the casserole dish—had I put it away somewhere different? Was I starting to suffer from Alzheimer's?

When my wife had moved out, while the girls and I were in England over the September school holidays, she told me that she would be taking "a few things" with her. Nothing major, she assured me, just a few personal items that were important to her and a few bits and pieces that would be helpful in setting up her new home. She also promised to leave me a list of everything she took and suggested that the rest of our possessions be divided between us as part of our settlement.

I wasn't really paying attention at the time; my mind was elsewhere, trying to convince her not to leave in the first place. And the reality was that I hadn't managed to work out what she had taken with her anyway. Firstly, because I didn't really know what we had and, secondly, because she didn't ever give me a list—apparently it would have been "too complicated". That was a hint, was it not?

The other factor contributing to my unease was that my wife still had a key to the house. She justified this on the basis that we both owned the house, which was true, and because it was important that she have access to the house in case the girls needed help and I was at work, or elsewhere, and couldn't get back. Or, if the girls were locked out, she would be able to let them in. This last point was not quite as compelling as my neighbours had a key for exactly that purpose, but it was good for the girls to know their mother was available should they need her, so I let it go.

Armed with her key, my wife had a rather annoying habit of letting herself into the house. She would take the courtesy of ringing the doorbell to announce her arrival and I would go to the front door, only to find her standing in the hallway or on her way to the kitchen. She thought this was fine as she had "rights" over the house, and I thought it was an invasion of my privacy.

So, all in all, I was becoming annoyed about her ability to access what I felt was my house whenever she liked and what appeared to be the gradual, stealthy removal of our possessions. I wasn't surprised that she refused to return her key and I was pretty sure that, even if she did, she would cut a spare one first.

In the lead up to our Gold Coast trip, I became increasingly worried about what might happen in the house while we were away. There was the risk of more 'unauthorised borrowing' and I also had various documents and my negotiating plans in regard to our financial settlement in my study. And I didn't want those falling into the wrong hands.

I wanted to change the locks but I wasn't sure whether it was legal. I spoke to the Legal Aid people about it. They told me property access is one of the most difficult and distressing issues that separated couples need to deal with. They also told me that it is a grey area—on the one hand my wife and I owned the house in joint names, and yet on the other hand I was paying the mortgage and rates and her residential address was elsewhere.

However, they also made me aware of a key principle under the law, namely that a person is entitled to 'peaceful occupation' of the property they live in—it's the same principle preventing a landlord from turning up unannounced and letting themself into a property they are renting out. Their conclusion was that, regardless of her joint ownership, my wife was not entitled to have free access to the house but that changing the locks could be construed as a step too far on my part. You've got to love the law—it's very hard to get a straight answer.

Despite the uncertainty and the greyness of the law, I went ahead and changed the locks. If my wife caused a legal scene I could always plead ignorance and give her a new key and at least I would be able to go on holiday and not worry about what might be happening in my house.

I felt a little awkward as I gave the girls their new house keys. I couldn't think of a plausible reason why I had changed the locks without telling them that I didn't trust their mother. So I decided honesty was the best approach.

"Girls, I'm afraid I have changed the locks and you need a new house key," I said.

"Why?" A simple question in return.

"I'm a bit worried about your mum coming into the house while we are away and going through my things."

"Yeah, that's probably right," said Sophie. "Mum sometimes borrows something when she comes in after dropping us back from dance if you're not around. She said it was okay with you."

Honesty was clearly the best policy and I felt vindicated by my decision. I felt even more vindicated when I received a phone call from my wife while I was on the Gold Coast. She wasn't happy.

"You've changed the locks, you arsehole." She was steaming with rage.

"How do you know that?" I replied, trying to be as calm as possible. Could I hear the sound of a truck in the background?

It was a question she couldn't answer. I knew she was on the doorstep trying to get into the house. And she knew that I knew it. There wasn't much she could do apart from insult me.

"You're an arsehole."

At least she was consistent.

The locks issue really got up her nose. When I next saw her a few weeks later, she hit me with her water bottle and then emptied it over my head.

25

Money

When we were happily married my wife and I would, from time to time, have the odd disagreement about money. I imagine we had a fairly traditional financial relationship—I was primarily responsible for the earning of our money and she was primarily responsible for the spending of it. Most of the time this relationship was fine but every so often something would happen to cause a difference of opinion—the credit card balance would suddenly jump, an outrageously complicated and expensive (in my opinion) coffee machine would appear in the kitchen, or my shirts would be taken out of the wardrobe to make way for some new dresses.

This would be the spark for a 'robust discussion', sometimes involving a bit of shouting and sometimes involving a few choice words that would need to be taken back later. But, regardless of the scale of the disagreement, the discussion would inevitably end up with one of two possible conclusions: The first, that my wife had actually saved us money by buying items that were on sale (in her view this was a positive thing—the more you spend, the more you save), so why was I being so unreasonable? Or the second, that I was a miserable tight-fisted bastard who needed to understand how much quality cost.

Whichever conclusion was reached, the argument would eventually pass and there would be the bonus of make-up sex at some point later that day, week or month—the timing would simply depend on the intensity of the argument, which in turn determined the intensity of the sex. It was all just part of life's rich pattern and the price that you, literally, pay for a working marriage.

You can imagine, therefore, the damage caused by a disagreement at the end of a marriage over every single dollar of money that you have, not to mention all of the possessions you have accumulated over a lifetime. The stakes are high. This is not a minor tiff; this is all about how much each of you is going to walk away with. The amounts are large, a lawyer is involved and there is no prospect of make-up sex, either with or without the lawyer. It's simply one of the greatest sources of conflict known to humankind. Once the love has gone and you are no longer on the same side—in fact you are now on opposite sides—it's a fight to the death.

The arguments we had over who was entitled to how much money and which bits of furniture, and who should pay for which future costs, dwarfed everything—including making sure that the children were coping with the impact of our split. If you want to drive a nail into the heart of a marriage and destroy any chance of reconciliation, simply start the financial settlement process and get a lawyer involved. I guarantee it will work every time.

Lawyers can make life unpleasant for you. But dealing with them is like facing a bouncer in a game of cricket. If you duck it, it can't get you out. Lawyers, like fast bowlers, try to frighten you and soften you up so that you either surrender or do something stupid, and give your wicket away. They write scary letters. I was told that I had "insufficient funds to stay in the house" and therefore it "should be sold at the soonest opportunity"; and that my actions were "unreasonable" and "inappropriate". (Me behaving inappropriately? I wasn't the one who had been screwing around behind my partner's back.) But ultimately a lawyer can't force you to do anything—they are not the law—only a Court can force you do something. And it takes a long time to get a matrimonial dispute to Court.

My wife and her lawyer could huff and puff all they liked, but I was in my house with my children and there was nothing they could do about it. The only rules were (1) we had to be separated for at least a year before we could get divorced and (2) if one of us wanted to go to the Family Court to resolve our financial settlement we needed to do so within twelve months of our divorce. That meant, according to my logic, I had up to two years to decide what was best for me and the children before I was compelled to act. Provided, of course, that I could keep my nerve. It was stressful, but as long as I kept reassuring myself that their words couldn't hurt me, I was okay. It was a great time to play the game like Geoff Boycott.

Dealing with my wife was a difficult exercise. She was very aggressive and, from my perspective, very unreasonable about what she wanted (a lot) and when she wanted it (immediately). But in some ways the hardest thing was that the woman with whom I had built my, in fact *our*, life with, was now my biggest enemy. I got to the point where I couldn't take her calls. I looked at her number on my mobile and let her go to voicemail. I would then steel myself, listen to her message and either ignore it or call her back after having had a chance to think. The problem of taking her calls was that I didn't know what frame of mind she would be in—abusive or constructive—and what she wanted to talk about. I didn't like being caught unprepared, so the best approach was to listen to her message, reflect on it and then call her back. This was far better for me than acting in the heat of the moment and saying something stupid.

We couldn't agree on anything. She wanted 60 percent of our financial assets. I was only prepared to give her 50 percent—why is it always the man who is deemed to be 'giving' money to his ex-wife? She wanted more of our money because she earned less than I did and because her other separated female friends typically got over 50 percent. My argument was that her separated female friends had equal or majority custody of their children and she didn't, so she should be grateful to have 50 percent. We were never going to agree and we both became more and more self-righteous and entrenched in our positions. It wasn't pretty. I once went through a whole mobile phone battery during one argument. It was exhausting.

We needed someone to help us find a fair solution and I thought there were a number of constructive ways of doing this. My wife, however, took a rather more extreme view—she decided to take me to Court. She was adamant a Court would see her side of the argument and that she would get what was rightfully hers. She also delighted in telling me that she had added a hard-arsed barrister to her legal team and that he was going to teach me a lesson and fuck me up. Could barristers do that? Was it legal? I wasn't sure, but I was actually a little bit scared. I had a vision of Vinnie Jones wearing a set of barrister's robes, "Oi son, come here. I want a little word with you…"

Regardless of the threat of a legal rogering, it did mean we were now on a timeline and that our ongoing arguments would eventually come to an end. It also meant that I needed to get my own lawyer. I remembered my school days and being involved in the classic five-year-old boy encounter:

"You stood on my soldier. I'm going to tell my dad and he's going to get you."

"Oh yeah? Well my dad's bigger than your dad, and he's going to get your dad."

Repeat ad infinitum. Escalate using other family members as required.

Hopefully my lawyer was bigger than her lawyer. It was just like being back in the playground—except a little more expensive.

I liked my lawyer. We had some good conversations. She told me things would be fine and that it was highly unlikely we would end up in Court (it takes forever to get a date and it's very expensive). She also confirmed, to my relief, that under the current legal system, a barrister can't actually fuck you up, although they will try and intimidate you. She made me feel a lot better about my situation and I had to resist the temptation to talk to her, or go and see her, too frequently because she had an annoying habit of sending me a bill every month. Each bill on its own wasn't too bad—but they were starting to add up. Don't use your lawyer for therapy. You might think that they like you and enjoy spending time with you listening to your delightful conversation, but they will still send you a bill.

My lawyer also told me that the legal process is nothing like an episode of *LA Law*, as my wife seemed to believe, and advised me to read various documents and a couple of sections of the Family Law Act. This is a long legal document of some 550 pages. It isn't a very entertaining read and I wouldn't recommend it as a holiday book but, as I'm a bit anal, I actually skimmed through most of it.

One section seemed to be at the heart of our disagreement and explained the various factors that the Court takes into account when splitting assets between waring ex-spouses. There were a lot—but there were only three that applied to us and, I suspect, to most divorcing couples. One—who earns, or is capable of earning, the most; two—who is responsible for the children; and three—does either party live with a new partner and therefore have additional financial support?

This made all the complexity seem quite straightforward. I was ahead 2–1. I had two factors in my favour—(i) I was responsible for the children on pretty much a full-time basis and (ii) my wife was living with her high-earning soul mate. The fact that I earned more than my wife would count against me. All in all, I felt this supported my idea of a 50/50 split of our financial assets and I couldn't see how my wife was justified in her claim for 60 percent.

Armed with my new legal knowledge I became even more annoying. I would quote random sections of the Family Law Act to my wife. I would reference sections and sub points, I would use phrases such as 'sub-judice' and 'case precedence' and 'ipso facto' and 'bah humbug'. I had no idea whether these phrases were correct, whether I was using them in the right context, or even whether they meant anything at all. But then neither did my wife, and so my Rumpole of the Bailey impression achieved two things. Firstly, it drove her mad and, secondly, she had to keep going back to her lawyer to check whether what I was saying was relevant—and this cost her money. All's fair in love and war!

My lawyer was impressed by my new found enthusiasm for, and understanding of, the law—although she did look a little blank when I tried out some of my legal phrases on her. We agreed that a 50/50 split of the financial assets would be our position. My wife was having none of it. Her lawyer had told her not to settle for less than 60 percent and so we were still stuck at square one. This was a better position for me than for her. I was the one living in the house and so was in no rush to find a solution. I battened down the hatches, reverted to Geoff Boycott mode, and waited.

I didn't need to wait too long. I received a summons, a polite letter inviting me and my wife to have a little chat with a judge. We were going to Court and, just to make it interesting, my wife now wanted 70 percent of our financial assets. It wasn't a nice letter and it did make my bottom quiver a little with nerves. But again, my lawyer was reassuring. She told me it would only be an initial hearing and we would ask to go to mediation so that the Court would not be bothered by our grubby little matter i.e. we would play for time.

A month or so later, like a nervous young footballer, I made my debut in Court. I decided to wear a suit—which, on arriving at the Court, I realised was the preferred look of the dodgy felon. I felt like a fully paid up member of the 'guilty party' fraternity. But at least my tie was done up properly and I hadn't borrowed my suit from a mate with a roughly similar, but not really the same, body shape. It was a very formal occasion with me, my wife, the judge and a couple of lawyers. I couldn't help thinking that the last time we had stood together at a legally based 'ceremony', we were getting married. It was almost perfect symmetry.

Our hearing lasted all of five minutes. It was like going to see the headmaster after being caught carving your name into a school desk. I felt extremely subservient. The case was adjourned and, as my lawyer had predicted, we were off to mediation. My wife and I didn't acknowledge each other's presence, or even make eye contact. We left the Court from different exits—again the exact opposite of our previous legally binding ceremony when we had arrived separately but left together.

I was feeling better about things. The spectre, and cost, of two days in Court had been lifted. I wasn't too worried about being grilled by a barrister—I thought I had a good case—I was more concerned by my lawyer's warning that the Court will often find in favour of the woman, regardless of the specific circumstances. In her view, the 50/50 split I wanted was likely to be my best-case outcome from a Court hearing, and, if we had a bad day, it could be a lot worse. Far better, she told me, to go to mediation and negotiate a good settlement. A good plan—although as it turned out not as straightforward as I hoped. It reminded me of a trip to Cairo.

A slight digression. Many years previously, when I was working in the UK, I managed a consulting project in Egypt. The team and I stayed in Cairo for a month or so and one weekend we decided to go and see the Pyramids. We had been warned a number of times by Fouadd, who ran our local office in Cairo, of the dangers of getting ripped-off in Egypt. To keep us safe, he kindly offered the services of his full-time driver. The driver would find us an 'official' guide so we would be certain of paying the 'official' price for a tour of the Pyramids (apparently you have to pay a guide for this—you can't just wander around by yourself and have a picnic). Great, it would be a Prince Charles type tour, we would be looked after and protected from the unofficial rip-off merchants.

We arrived at the Pyramids in some style, cosseted in Fouadd's big, black Mercedes. True to his word, Fouadd's driver took us to the "best Pyramids guide in the whole of Cairo". The conversation went something like this:

"I have been sent by Fouadd. He has asked me to find the best Pyramids guide in the whole of Cairo to take his three friends and colleagues on a tour of the Pyramids that they will never forget," the driver proclaimed, very grandly.

"My friend, today the Gods have looked down upon you and smiled," replied the guide. "For I am the best Pyramids guide in the whole of Cairo and I will devote myself to your service.

I will give you the best tour of the Pyramids. Because Fouadd has sent you, I will do this on horseback and for a special price. And, because you are my friends, I will take you to a special place, forbidden to tourists. It will be an unforgettable experience."

There was much arm waving from the legendary guide.

"You are so gracious," replied the driver. "May I ask what the special price will be?"

"Ten Egyptian pounds per horse!" the guide thundered.

It was about $25 each. I thought I heard some onlookers take sharp intakes of breath, but I can't be sure.

"Indeed, that is a special price," the driver gasped, in some kind of wonderment.

It was all a bit dramatic but good theatre and we felt that we had a good deal. Going round the Pyramids on horseback did seem a bit special, plus we would also have a trip to the special place, forbidden to tourists.

"Come, let us find our fine Arabic horses!!" the guide proclaimed.

We mounted our fine Arabic horses, which appeared to be the geriatric parents of the knackered, old donkeys, which, as a child, I used to ride on Blackpool beach. Actually, to say I rode them is a bit of an overstatement—in reality I was towed along by a bloke walking beside the donkey. And it was the same here in Cairo. The three of us sat on our donkeys, which were joined by a long rope to the guide, who was riding his own, albeit slightly younger, donkey.

As our donkey train made its way across the short piece of sand separating the Pyramids from metropolitan Cairo, it became obvious that all the tourists were, in fact, riding on "fine Arabic horses" being towed by a guide. Clearly, this was similar to the "you must hire a buggy" rule when playing golf in the United States. Our tour wasn't so extraordinary after all—however we did have our visit to the special place, forbidden to tourists, to look forward to.

Although I sound cynical it was quite neat going round the Pyramids, even though there were a fair few donkeys to navigate (but no worse than Chadstone car park on a busy Saturday). The Pyramids are extraordinary structures. We didn't learn a lot from our guide though, partly because he was at the head of our donkey train, partly because his English wasn't very good, but mostly because he couldn't be bothered to tell us anything. At one point he became quite animated and waved his hands in the direction of a small pile of distant rocks. I thought I may have heard the phrase "special place, forbidden to tourists", as we passed.

Tour over; our guide towed us back to the starting point. We dismounted and I paid the guide thirty Egyptian pounds, as we had agreed. He shook his head.

"This is not enough," he looked at me, shaking his head, as though I had wronged his entire family.

"We agreed a price of ten pounds per horse," I replied, genuinely confused.

"We did—ten pounds per horse. That is ten pounds for each of your horses and ten pounds for my horse. It is forty pounds."

I couldn't fault his logic and these were, technically, the terms of our verbal contract. I paid him the forty pounds with a slight smile on my face. We had been had—but in quite a clever way.

So what is the point of this digression?

When I left the main story, I was pleased that my wife and I were going to mediation, rather than a Court hearing, to settle our differences. This was a good thing; it was going to be a lot more cost effective and likely to produce a better outcome for me.

I imagined mediation may actually be like an episode of *LA Law* —a smart boardroom, me and my lawyer on one side of the table, my wife and her lawyer on the other, a small tray of water, coffee and some chockie biscuits in the middle. But no. This was mediation Court style. My lawyer explained that we would need to get a barrister to negotiate on our behalf. My barrister would go head to head with my wife's barrister—a kind of my dad is bigger than your dad arrangement. My lawyer would also need to attend to advise on points of law and to make sure that whatever was agreed was documented properly. So that was now a lawyer and a barrister on each side.

But it didn't end there; my lawyer also explained that a third barrister would be required. He would act as the mediator and help us reach an agreement. My wife and I would go halves on his costs. For a moment I was back in Egypt. How many horses was I paying for? It seemed a bit over the top and crowded, after all this wasn't a major legal drama, it was just me and my wife not being able to agree over money.

"It will be very cosy around the negotiating table," I said to my lawyer.

"Don't worry," she replied. "You won't see your wife and her legal team. It's too emotional and intimidating for people. We will sit in one room and they will be in another. The mediating barrister will move between the two rooms and broker an agreement."

This all seemed crazy and expensive to me. But that is exactly what happened. My lawyer and I went to see my newly appointed barrister and I briefed him on my argument. Ker Ching! I met him again the day before mediation to agree a plan of attack. Ker Ching! We went to Court and I spent the whole day with my lawyer, my barrister and the mediating barrister. Double Ker Ching!

The mediation process was not exactly action packed. There was a lot of waiting around, punctuated by moments of pure adrenaline—there was a lot at stake, after all. It reminded me of watching a Formula One Grand Prix. It's dangerous but mostly boring, albeit with the occasional moment of great excitement.

To begin with nothing happened. I sat with my legal team in our allotted room for an hour making small talk. The most expensive small talk of my life. I watched the clock tick round—beating out the cost per second. We were then summoned to a big room along with my wife and her legal team. The mediating barrister gave a little speech. He sounded like the referee at the start of a boxing match—let's have a good, clean fight, no punching below the belt, etc., etc. We then went back to our own rooms. The mediating barrister took my barrister out for an hour. I waited with my lawyer. My barrister came back and, rather cryptically, said everything would be fine and that we would reach agreement. The three of us waited for another hour. Nothing happened—except my bill kept ticking up.

Eventually the mediating barrister returned.

"I have an offer for you," he announced, very solemnly.

I held my breath. I had a mental flash of a fat Egyptian sitting on a donkey. My heart was racing. Here it comes, how bad is it going to be? The mediating barrister cleared his throat.

"The other side is prepared for you to keep the family home, provided that you agree to a 50/50 split of all the financial assets including the house, superannuation and pension balances, and a 50/50 split of the furniture and chattels," the barrister intoned. He paused. "I will leave you to think about it."

I was lost for words. I didn't know whether to be happy or angry. The phrase "that was what I fucking offered her months ago" came to mind. Were they serious? Had these last six months of pain and stress just been a bluff to try and get me to agree to something unreasonable?

I looked at my barrister. He shrugged.

"Your wife had an unreasonable expectation," he said. "Her barrister knew it and now the mediator has confirmed it."

"Should I burst into their room, bang on the table, shout a bit, use some of my legal phrases and give her the bill for the mediation?" I asked.

"That wouldn't be particularly helpful in my view," my barrister replied, poker faced.

Lighten up mate, it was only a joke.

So that was that. It was all done within a few hours. We then spent the rest of the day agreeing some other big conditions. I would pay for the school fees and medical costs, she would pay for dance costs—and nitpicking over the smaller bits; my wife had a list of the furniture she wanted.

I was oblivious to most of this. I had got what I wanted and was bursting with relief and happiness. I had kept the house at a good price and could just about afford the payment I was required to make to my wife. It had been a brilliant day and a perfect reward for all the hard work I had put into mine and the girls' lives. I celebrated with another Tim Henman-style fist pump.

When I got home, I had a long bath and a well-earned glass of red. It was the end of an emotional and tiring few months and our financial settlement represented a major milestone in our separation process. I was exhausted and relieved, the kind of feeling you get after finishing a set of exams, knowing that you have done your best. My relaxation was interrupted by my mobile ringing. It was my wife. Was she going to give me another set of verbals? Was she going to tell me that the agreement was now off? No, she wanted to share how she felt. How worn out she was. How glad she was that the fighting was over. How pleased she was that we could now get on with our lives and rebuild our relationship. It was weird. Two heavyweight boxers embracing after a 15-round slugfest during which they had been trying to destroy each other.

But she was wrong. The fighting wasn't over. It wasn't over then and it isn't over today as I write this. I doubt if it will ever be completely over, it just gets less intense and less frequent as time passes.

The next step in our fighting, fortunately outside of Court but still requiring the lawyers, was to agree a Child Support Agreement i.e. to formalise who would pay for which of the children's costs. This was less critical for me as I was paying the majority of their costs anyway.

It took a few more months to reach agreement. I don't know why because it wasn't very complicated—just emotional. My wife and I soon went back to arguing over money, the problems I was causing by not encouraging the girls to live with her, the fact that I wasn't buying enough clothes for them and so on, and on, and on. My wife, understandably, wanted more control over the lives of our children. They lived with me and I was responsible for them financially and also for helping them to rebuild their lives. A difficult position for her to be in. She didn't have much choice but to stand on the sidelines and throw rocks at my parenting.

The girls were over the moon when I told them we would be keeping the house. It was a great outcome for them. They didn't want to move. Staying in our home, with all its familiarity and comfort, provided a great piece of stability and reassurance. It was a good day for them too. Annabel celebrated by repeating her trick of writing "We Love Dad" across the family room windows. Yet again she unfortunately used the wrong marker pen. It came off eventually—but it was great while it was up there, a permanent reminder of her feelings.

The financial settlement was long and tough. I learned a lot during the process. I have included some of my learning points at the end of the book.

26

D-i-v-o-r-c-e

According to the Law a married couple have to be separated for twelve months before they can begin divorce proceedings. On day 366 post-separation, I had to wait an extra day because it was a leap year, I had the forms filled in. All I had to do was to get my wife to sign them—if she did then ours would be treated as an agreed divorce; if she didn't then I would need to go to Court to have the marriage annulled. I thought it would be bit cheeky of her if she didn't agree to sign them.

Despite everything we had been through, filling in the divorce application was a difficult and emotional job. A very clinical end to our relationship. But my wife had been living with another man for a year—so what choice did I have? It wasn't as if she was living around the corner on her own and there was a possibility of reconciliation. She was another man's partner. I had my pride. I couldn't stay married for a day longer than I had to under these circumstances.

I sent the forms to my wife for her to sign and asked her to go halves in the $400 application fee. She was prepared to sign the forms, but refused to share in the cost. She told me she couldn't afford it and that I was "rushing the divorce through"—and so if I wanted a divorce I would have to pay for it. Never did quite understand that logic.

A few months later I received a nice certificate from the Federal Magistrates Court. It was very brief, stark and matter of fact. A single sentence saying that our marriage, solemnised on 11 August 1990, was over. I read it a number of times. It was terribly final. And because the certificate mentioned the date of our marriage, the day itself came flooding back to me.

It was a hot day in August, I remembered getting ready with my brother and best man; the suits and tails we wore; my future wife coming down the aisle; saying our vows; drinking a bottle of sweet, warm champagne in the car on the way to the reception; my absolute disaster of a wedding speech (I thought I was hilarious, but apparently I was just rude); dancing with my nan; and dropping my trousers for comedic effect—I was obviously far too immature to get married. They were all good memories. And now a complete stranger, the Registrar of the Federal Magistrates Court, had ended it all. I took the certificate and filed it away along with the birth certificates, my marriage certificate and the dogs' worming certificates.

The next time I saw my wife, now ex-wife, she told me that she had also received the divorce certificate. I could tell she was a bit emotional about it, probably for the same reasons I was, except of course she could trace the beginnings of the process to end our marriage to her own actions.

"We are divorced," she said, standing on the doorstep and looking quite sad.

I knew that the right thing to do was to invite her in and spend a while reflecting on our seventeen years of marriage, how our lives had matured, the girls' early years, our time living in England, maybe even my dad's death. But I didn't.

"What did you expect would happen?" I said. "Surely this is

what you wanted? You are living with another man, how can we stay married? Bye."

I shut the door.

And that was that.

27

Perfect strangers

As all separated and divorced men know the relationship with your wife/ex-wife never ends, it just takes on a new form, some bits of which are good, and some bits not so good. My relationship with my ex is generally nondescript, punctuated with the occasional disagreement, argument, rude word, moment of pleasantness and outbreak of sweaty armpits.

If I had to pick a single word to describe our relationship, I would choose 'frustrating'. We rarely see each other or catch up on each other's news. I don't think that we will ever get on, partly because of the intensely painful way in which our marriage ended and partly because we still occasionally argue, mostly over money—and we never saw eye to eye on money when we were married, so how can we be expected to now that we are divorced? The easiest way forward for me is just to ignore her. I'm not saying that it's the right way forward but it's the way that works for me.

The other issue that has gone hand-in-hand with having my ex-wife in my life has been having her soul mate in my life. Or more accurately, trying to avoid having him in my life. From day one I decided, quite reasonably in my view, that I would never acknowledge him or speak to him. My logic was simple. He was the guy who had caused my family to be ripped apart.

If he had not come on the scene then my wife wouldn't have left me.

I accept that my stance has not made life any easier for my children. I am not prepared to share milestone events with him. In the early days of our separation, when I threw a thirteenth birthday party for Annabel, I was happy for my wife to attend but not the soul mate. I took the same approach to Sophie's eighteenth three years later, even though my now ex-wife put up a strong case for the soul mate being "part of their family unit" and for me "needing to move on". Maybe she was right, but I took offence to her lack of sensitivity in thinking that there shouldn't be any difficulty in my meeting him for the first time, in my house, at my daughter's eighteenth. Although this made life difficult for Sophie, she was caught in the crossfire of her parents arguing and lobbying her as to why/why not the soul mate should be invited, I wouldn't budge. I was prepared to compromise on many things but not this one, it was a matter of principle.

And besides, what would the soul mate and I talk about? The only thing we have in common appears to be my ex-wife, and it's clear we both have different views on that subject. I suppose I could ask him whether she still makes that strange grunting noise in the middle of the night, or whether he's able to cope with only having 10 percent of the available wardrobe space. I just can't see what else we would have to talk about.

My children did eventually meet the soul mate and, when they started to spend some time at their mother's house, they inevitably started to spend time with him as well. We rarely spoke about him but, ultimately, I couldn't help myself from asking them what he was like.

"He's quite nice, but nothing like you," they told me.

Was that what I wanted to hear? Would I have preferred

them to say that they couldn't stand him? Whether I liked it or not he was going to play some part, however small, in their lives. I grudgingly accepted it was better that they got on with him. On balance "quite nice" was probably a good outcome.

But perhaps the greatest reason for my complete indifference towards him was that he had won my wife. And that hurt. She had been prepared to sacrifice her relationship with our children to be with him. This wasn't a case of her having a slight preference for him over me. She had made a decision to turn the lives of her family (me, the girls, her parents and her wider family) on their heads, had risked alienating her friends and had moved out of her family home to be with him. That was a big call. She would only have done that if she had been barking mad or had concluded that her new soul mate was a much better and more fulfilling partner than I was—and I didn't think she was barking mad. If he was her Manchester United, then I must have been her Tranmere Rovers reserves.

There was an ego thing at play here. Any meeting or conversation that I might have with the soul mate would be underpinned by the subtext of my wife's decision to choose him over me. And I didn't think I could handle that. We wouldn't be able to interact as equals. I would feel that behind his eyes he would be thinking "she prefers me to you, loser".

Initially my selfish preference was for my ex-wife and her soul mate to break up. It's not that I wished my ex-wife to be unhappy, or on her own, and end up a lonely old woman living in a slightly mouldy apartment with a bunch of cats. Why would I want that? I would have just preferred that she met someone else and had a new soul mate. That way there would be no more of the "you chose him over me" issue and tension. I would be able to get on with, and talk to, the new man. We could go for a beer. I could sympathise with him when he confessed that she was driving him nuts ("yep, she did that to me too") and I could get him up to speed with what she likes in bed—a nice cup of tea and marmalade on toast, if you must know.

But hang on a minute. If she chose a new soul mate would I be even more inferior to the new one? Would it be a case of her finding a man who was better and more accomplished than the one she left me for? An iPod Touch to the original iPod Classic? A sort of super soul mate? Let's not go there. Let's just go with my daughters' description of "quite nice" and leave it at that.

28

Burn

With a year's worth of experience under my belt, I was now a lot better at being a father and at running the house. In fact, I would go as far as saying that I had it pretty much cracked. My routines were working well. The children were happy and settled. And I was feeling much better about myself and my life.

The biggest improvement by far was in my cooking capability. Looking back, I don't think it's fair to describe my early days of food production as cooking, in the traditional sense of the word. It was more a case of me heating things up in order. I was good at it, mind you, and the core components of my meals—a piece of meat/fish, the accompanying pasta/rice/potato and vegetables—were all ready at the same time. But my approach was more suited to passing a science practical exam than producing a good meal. My objective was to provide a specified number of elements on a plate, at the same time, with each being at an appropriate temperature.

The other common characteristic of my food could be summed up in a single word—'dryness'. Not in the *MasterChef* sense of some elements of a dish being dry to provide contrast to those elements that are moist or sweet. This was a more traditional definition of dryness, as in 'containing very little moisture'. Basically, I couldn't do sauce or gravy, and there was absolutely no prospect of me creating a tantalising jus. As a result, every meal I served up consisted of its core components only. It was a little limited.

Fortunately salvation was at hand and, out of the blue, I had an epiphany and things began to change. I watched a few minutes of Jamie Oliver on TV. I don't know which of his many shows it was but in the space of a short period of time I became strangely attracted to him. Here was an ordinary bloke who seemed to be able to cook without the need for too much precision or without being too fancy. He dealt in units that I could understand—handfuls and glugs and bits. Jamie was passionate, made cooking seem like fun and, more importantly, relatively straightforward.

On this particular program he was teaching what looked like a bunch of no-hoper men some basic skills—and it hit me that cooking may not be as difficult and as mystical as I had assumed. Maybe it wasn't something that women are genetically capable of doing and men are genetically designed to cock up. It even appeared as though it was actually possible for a man to do more than simply barbeque the buggery out of a piece of meat, or worse, a bunch of prawns.

To be honest, I didn't learn too much from my initial ten-minute exposure, but I did come away with a piece of culinary gold. The mighty Jamie showed the no-hopers how to make a simple tomato sauce which could be the basis for any dish. He fried an onion, poured a tin of diced tomatoes over it, simmered it for a while and added some salt and pepper. It was quick, easy and his studio guests were fawning all over it. I could do that.

And I did. We now had tomato sauce with everything—tuna with tomato sauce and pasta; lamb with tomato sauce, vegetables and rice; roast chicken with tomato sauce; spaghetti bolognaise with homemade tomato sauce; and salmon with tomato sauce and mashed potatoes (we only had that once, it wasn't a great combination).

And, because my regular cooking schedule always included a roast on Sunday evenings, I now had a perfect and efficient meal lined up for Mondays. I could serve up the leftover meat with a sauce (tomato, of course) and rice the following day.

The girls were very encouraging of my culinary advance. They told me how much they enjoyed the tomato sauce and how it "brightened up" my usual dry fare, but they also suggested there might be other sauces that I could add to my repertoire. And they were right. I had my second epiphany—I discovered recipe bases. There were loads of them—satay, Italian tomato (I didn't really need that one), red wine casserole, creamy Thai, apricot, stroganoff and many more. They each had a little set of instructions on the back that were easy to follow.

It was simple, all I had to do was fry some onion, brown the meat, add a few vegetables, maybe add a tin of tomatoes or some cream, chuck in the recipe base, simmer for a while and, voila, a bona fide meal. I was becoming a proper cook and it was good. The kids loved the fact that, finally, we now had some proper variety, and moisture, in our diet. Best of all, I could regularly turn out a meal in thirty minutes. And that became my rule for midweek cooking—if it couldn't be done in thirty minutes then it wasn't going to happen. Time was too important. (*I've subsequently noticed that Jamie has recently picked up on this theme, introduced the thirty minute meal into his own repertoire and is, no doubt, making a nice bit of dough from the books and associated TV program. I don't begrudge him this—it's great that we have a give and take relationship and can learn from each other. Nice one!*)

Once I started I couldn't stop. I was beginning to enjoy

putting the various elements of the meal together and I really loved frying things—watching the colours change, the sizzle and the smell. It was a schoolboy chemistry lab thing all over again, except without the regular, amusing stink of sulphur or sudden flares of burning magnesium.

I then did something I would never have anticipated in my wildest dreams—I opened a recipe book, Jamie Oliver, of course. My mum had bought me the book when she came to stay the previous year and it had remained in splendid isolation on my kitchen shelf, but now my lisping, fellow pom and I were going to become good mates. The book was a bit intimidating at first, some of the recipes looked quite complicated and contained ingredients I had never heard of and had no clue where to find. They required things like pearl barley, cardamom and cumin (which I initially thought was a joke ingredient, but that was largely because I was pronouncing it incorrectly) and involved folding and reducing. It was a big step up but one that I wanted to take. How hard could it be? I just needed to follow the instructions.

One Saturday, I took the plunge and entered Jamie's world. I decided to tackle an easier looking recipe, a dark lamb stew. I went to the butcher and greengrocer in the morning to buy the ingredients, picked some rosemary from the garden (which I imagined Jamie would fully approve of) and set to work. It was quite time consuming but good fun; there was a lot more chopping up and grinding of herbs and spices than in recipe-base land, but it was also a lot more satisfying. I was creating something. And, once it started cooking in the oven, the aroma was fantastic.

When the girls came home from dance they couldn't believe it.

"What's that smell?" asked Annabel.

"I'm doing a dark lamb stew for dinner," I announced, trying to appear casual.

They were impressed. Annabel performed five pirouettes around the kitchen, a sign of both approval and excitement.

It was great to have something in the oven, cooking itself, rather than having to stand over the frying pan which is much more labour intensive and requires more precision. I was able to retire to the lounge room with a celebratory glass of wine, although unfortunately this proved to be my undoing. Spurred on by my enthusiasm, my success at having a bubbling stew in the oven and the good vibe of the alcohol, I made the classic errors of (a) thinking that I had conquered the culinary world and (b) thinking that I knew more about this particular dish than Jamie.

I had a few carrots and mushrooms in the stew, as per the recipe, and I decided to add in my greens as well, rather than cooking them separately. I imagined that they would absorb the flavours of the stew and be tastier as a result. So, in a grand off-piste moment, I chucked some broccoli in. It wasn't a major mistake but one that would take the gloss off the finished product somewhat. I was blissfully unaware of this though—I was back on the sofa with my wine.

An hour later, it was time for the unveiling of the stew. I carefully took the pot out of the oven using my oven gloves—what a versatile piece of equipment they are—and put it on the cook top. The girls gathered around me, eager to witness the new dawn of my enhanced culinary capability. They were excited. I was excited.

I took off the lid.

"Ta-dah!" I proclaimed.

"Ew," said Sophie.

"What the hell is that?" I heard Annabel whisper to herself.

I remember seeing a flash of something green as I removed the lid of the pot, but I couldn't concentrate on the stew at that moment—I had more pressing matters to deal with. The lid had welded itself to my hand. In my enthusiasm to create a Hollywood style unveiling moment I had forgotten to use the oven gloves when I took the lid off. It had been nicely heated to 180 degrees.

"You absolute sodding bastard of a thing," I screamed, as I poured cold water over my branded hand. God, it was painful.

"It's not that bad, Dad," said Sophie. "It just looks a bit unusual." The girls were still focussed on the stew, oblivious to my pain.

I regained my composure and peered back into the pot. After a good hour of bubbling away, the broccoli had completely disintegrated and created a green film on the top of the stew. It looked disconcertingly like a skanky old pond with slime floating on it. My chipolatas were making a brave effort to break through the green crust. They looked like little turds from a sewage pipe floating in a septic river. However, despite its uninviting looks, it smelt fantastic.

Annabel summed it up quite well. "It's a shame that you eat with your eyes," she said. That girl watches too much *MasterChef*.

Fortunately it tasted as good as it smelt, so we just turned the lights down and ate in the semi-darkness to negate the 'eat with your eyes' concept, the gentle red glow emanating from my hand supplementing the atmosphere.

I was very happy with my progression from total beginner to a full-on cook from scratch capability. I gradually became more adventurous and tried other Jamie dishes, normally with good results. However, after the broccoli incident I vowed never again to deviate from the recipe—I was precise with my volumes and cooking times, to the millilitre and second where possible. The keys to successful cooking became apparent to me—a good recipe, good ingredients, planning and discipline. When I cook I only cook. There is no multi-tasking and there is no last minute change to the plan or ingredients. I still adopt a pseudo 'chemistry lab session' approach to my cooking but it seems to work. It's really not as hard as you might think, and here's a tip—it impresses family and the ladies enormously.

Eventually, I discovered there can be a bit of flexibility in cooking main courses and that flexibility can be fun. But for baking and desserts precision is critical. It's like making love—a bit of variety is good from time to time, but don't stray too far from the basics or you risk losing your audience.

29

Who's that girl?

The other major step forward in our life together was my daughters getting more involved in running the house. The girls were good at doing one-off tasks when I asked them to, such as unloading the dishwasher or picking up some vegetables from the fruit shop, but nothing happened on a regular basis. I pretty much had to ask for help every time I needed it. Although they rarely said no, I didn't want to have to keep on asking them. I wanted them to help me out without being asked.

I thought about basing payment of their pocket money on the completion of jobs but chose not to as I thought my daughters should feel a commitment to the household that was not tied to financial reward. I needed them to understand that the house didn't run itself and that we all had our roles to play. Plus, as Annabel had told me quite eloquently, "I don't need pocket money because you buy me everything I need".

It took a bit of time and some gentle reminders. The girls had different views to mine on the importance of keeping the house clean and tidy and what an acceptable standard was. But we got there eventually. They became responsible for doing their own washing, vacuuming and keeping their rooms tidy, cleaning their bathroom, emptying the dishwasher and picking up odds and ends from the shops on their way home from school. It worked well and they took some pride in their work, although they would also adopt a 'hear no evil, see no evil' approach to certain tasks. For example, if they found a mouldy apple core in their bin they were unable to touch it, "it's too gross", and so would leave it until it had grown a lovely head of furry hair, completely taking over the bottom of the bin. I would then be called in to perform a professional recovery operation.

But it wasn't all smooth progress. There were still issues to deal with and one of the most challenging was picking up my eldest from parties that seemed to end later and later. I couldn't keep going to get her from parties once the finish time crept beyond midnight. It was just too hard—I either had to stay up by myself until collection time, or go to bed and then wake up in time to do the pick up—and I needed my sleep. The final straw proved to be a fairly daunting, long distance pick up at three in the morning. On the way home, with a group of girls laughing and singing in the back of the car and the radio blaring out some crappy, doof-doof techno thing in the front, I resolved that enough was enough. Myself and a number of other parents agreed that we would start to encourage the girls to share cabs home.

Although this was a step forward in some respects, I now had to convince myself to go to sleep even though my eldest was still out partying. It wasn't easy. I would normally go to bed, sleep for about an hour, and then lie awake waiting to hear her key in the door. I might have been in bed, but I still wasn't getting any sleep.

There were also times when I would fall sleep, only to wake up in the early hours of the morning wondering whether she was back. I would then get out of bed, go upstairs and check her bedroom to see if she had returned. On one such occasion, I woke up in the middle of the night thinking I had heard footsteps upstairs. I lay in bed for a few minutes but didn't hear any other sounds. I tried to go back to sleep but, because I wasn't sure whether Sophie was home, I knew this would be impossible until I had checked.

I sleep naked. This isn't because I am in love with my own body, but simply because I don't like the feel of pyjamas close to my skin and I find I get a bit tangled up if I wear them. If I'm honest, my nocturnal nudity is one of the factors behind my oven glove requirement. So, when I performed my night-time patrols upstairs, I needed to put my undies on and grab my dressing gown.

On this particular evening I stepped into my undies but, as it was a warm night, didn't bother with my dressing gown. I got to the foot of the stairs and looked up. The house was dark and I couldn't see or hear anyone. I decided to go up the stairs to check. Halfway up I saw Sophie in the darkness, standing outside the bathroom. Good, she's home, I thought, and I took a few more steps up the stairs so that I could give her a goodnight kiss.

Sophie didn't say anything as I approached which I didn't find strange—I just assumed that she couldn't see me in the dark. Happy she was home, I had almost reached the top of the stairs when the bathroom door opened and both I, and the person I was heading towards, were bathed in light. It was a bright light and, because my eyes were accustomed to the dark, I instinctively put my hands across them. As I squinted through my fingers my stomach dropped. It was Sophie who had come out of the bathroom and therefore the person at the top of the stairs was not in fact my daughter, but one of her friends. And I was now standing near the top of the stairs, bathed in light, wearing only my undies and with my hands up around my head. I doubted whether this was a good look.

Within a microsecond, and again instinctively, I took my hands from my head and, in a brilliant impression of Michael Jackson, grabbed the front of my undies in a bid to cover myself up. It was horribly awkward. I almost fell as I turned on the stairs and rushed down them, blurting a hurried and inane apology over my shoulder.

"Was that your dad?" I heard Sophie's friend ask.

"Yep."

"What was he doing?"

"Dunno."

"Was he…?"

"No. Don't be stupid," my daughter replied, as they both started laughing.

I jumped back into bed feeling a mixture of shame and embarrassment. I didn't sleep well that night; I was half expecting to see the torches of the posse through my bedroom window.

Sophie and I both agreed that we needed to prevent unfortunate episodes of this type from occurring again. We devised a simple scheme. I would leave the front porch light on and she would turn if off when she came in. That way, to make sure she was home, I would only need to check whether the light was off rather than go upstairs. It was a good plan.

I have to confess that, unfortunately, the 'up the stairs' incident was repeated at a later date although this time it involved a different friend, which I think makes it a bit better. Sophie has pointed out to me that once can be excused, twice can be considered an accident, but a third time might be construed as something worse. She is right. If I think I hear footsteps upstairs, I now send her a text.

30

Love shack

Meanwhile, Alison and I continued with our well-practiced routine of seeing each other at the weekend and occasionally during the week. It was a routine that fitted in well with bringing up our children but it was becoming more and more frustrating—our life together was fragmented and becoming harder to deal with as the depth of our feelings for each other grew.

We were, however, on the verge of what would be a significant change in our living arrangements. Alison's former husband had returned from New Zealand and they agreed that their boys should spend more time with him. The boys moved to a schedule where they had alternate weeks with each parent. One week with Dad and one week with Mum, which seems to be an increasingly common arrangement for children of separated parents.

This was a real challenge for Alison. It was hard for her to let her boys go, even though she knew it was the right thing to do. I received a phone call from Alison the moment after the boys had been collected to start the first week at their father's house. She was very distressed. Alison had been their primary carer for over eight years and now felt as though the boys had suddenly moved out of home. She was struggling with a huge sense of loss. But, while this change in routine was difficult for

Alison to adjust to, it also gave us more freedom to develop our own relationship.

I was now able to see a lot more of Alison. She spent increasing amounts of time at my house during the weeks that the boys were with their father. This helped her to gradually build her relationship with my girls. She began to come round to my house for dinner on a regular basis and spend the evening with us. Sometimes she would stay the night, and sometimes she would go back home.

It was great having Alison in the house. In the early days she was very much my guest and she behaved herself. I would sit her down with a glass of wine in front of the fire and she would stay there. I would cook her dinner and she would be grateful for it, eat it and help with the clearing up. But, as she began to feel more at home, her female desire to 'contribute' began to kick in. One evening we were having a drink and talking, as normal, and I went to the loo, also as normal—I've got the bladder of a small child. But this time when I came back into the lounge room I found Alison with a duster in her hand, attacking my mantelpiece.

On another occasion she went to the loo herself and, after five minutes, hadn't returned. I waited patiently. I was curious. I didn't want to rush her on the basis that she might have become so comfortable in my home, she was now relaxed enough to nip off and do some major business. But after another five minutes had passed I began to wonder whether something was wrong. Surely this wasn't a reprise of the 'something that she ate' episode? I knocked gently on the bathroom door.

"Are you alright in there?" I asked quietly.

"I'm fine," she replied.

I could hear what sounded like water being sloshed around. I hesitated.

"I'll be out in a minute," she added.

I went back into the lounge room and waited. A couple of minutes later she rejoined me, looking very pleased with herself, but offering no explanation for the time that she'd been gone. We carried on talking.

Later, on my way to the kitchen, I stuck my head into the bathroom. I noticed that the towels had been folded neatly and put back symmetrically on the towel rail; the mirror looked as though it had been wiped down; the sink looked cleaner; and there was a faint smell of Toilet Duck in the air. I wasn't sure what had happened. Either Alison had suffered an enormous intestinal expulsion, which had necessitated a major bathroom clean-up operation or, more likely, she had decided that my bathroom was not up to standard.

As Alison being in the house became more normal, she started to take on a little more of the household management. She would sometimes come round before I got home so that she could get on with dinner. She began to buy the odd thing from the supermarket, clean the benchtops, run the vacuum cleaner around and so on. It was great to have the domestic support and it started to change the nature of our relationship. We were moving from a purely dating relationship to one that also included some practical, day-to-day stuff. This was a good thing—our relationship was deepening as a result and, from a selfish point of view, my life was getting easier.

Over a period of six months we eventually reached a point where Alison largely moved in and lived with me and the girls when her boys were with their father, and then lived back in her own house when the boys were with her. And with this change she took on more and more responsibility. She took over the midweek cooking role, her cleaning and tidying up regime broadened, and she became an integral part of the fabric of our lives.

It was a good arrangement to road-test our relationship. It meant that I had a week with Alison and my girls and then a week with just the girls. It gave my children a chance to get used to Alison without her being with us on a full-time basis. It was a gradual, rather than sudden, change.

Ironically, the person who was most impacted by these living arrangements was Alison herself. She had to adjust to packing clothes and the things she needed for work when she came to stay with me, keep running back to her house when she needed something extra and generally put up with the inconvenience of living in two houses. She was effectively living the same week-about routine as her children—and she found it a complete pain. I wonder whether if more parents experienced this lifestyle for themselves they would be less inclined to inflict it on their children.

Mind you, these new arrangements were not without some minor controversy. The girls and I had our own standards of cleanliness and we liked the way we did things. I knew that we weren't the tidiest family in the world but I thought we were pretty good. We kept the communal areas to a high, agreed, standard but our bedrooms were our own domains and our 'house rule' was that we could manage these according to our own, individual, standards. Alison had a slightly more 'open for inspection' approach to household management. She liked things to be neat or, as a minimum, perfect.

As our lives together progressed, I noticed that Alison would double up with me on some tasks and also re-clean things that I had already cleaned. For example, I would make the bed and she would re-make it slightly differently, with a more uniform pillow alignment. Did she think I wouldn't notice? This was quite entertaining when Alison was only in the house a few times a week but, as she began to spend more time with us, I thought that we should agree some new ground rules—or else there was a risk we would both end up getting frustrated and annoyed with each other. I felt I was wasting my time doing jobs if Alison was going to do them again later. Alison, no doubt, was thinking that the reason she needed to re-do the job was because I hadn't done it properly in the first place, or at least properly as she defined it.

However, I couldn't just stop doing my household jobs completely. I didn't want Alison to presume I was happy for her to take over my workload and that I had washed my hands of my household chores. That felt a bit old school to me. I didn't see her as my 'domestic helper' and I didn't want her to think that this was her new role. So I continued to do bits of housework and she continued to 'correct' my efforts. It was all a bit silly.

Maybe evolution was to blame. Let me explain. When I was married I had a very minor domestic role. My wife had set the standards and rules for our household chores. I didn't have a view on the subject. I fitted in with the way she liked things done and complied. We evolved together. It just seemed to be the natural thing to do. But as a single father I had taken on full domestic responsibilities. I performed these tasks in a way, and to a standard, that fitted in with the other demands in my life—looking after the girls, going to work, trying to get laid, etc. My approach worked for me—it was another form of evolution.

With Alison things were different. We hadn't evolved together. We had come together suddenly and we had different ways of doing things. And we both thought our way was best, or in my case, satisfactory. Similar to my wife, Alison was used to setting the domestic living rules, had her own standards and expected compliance. And, due to my time on my own, I now had my own rules and standards. I decided that we needed to talk about it before these differences formed a blight on our relationship. Something had to give. We couldn't continue to live together having different standards, we needed to find some common ground—we managed it, but it took a while.

Fortunately, there was more to life than domestic chores. We still managed to have our fair share of fun. In fact, on my birthday, Alison blew the needle on the fun meter right off the dial—she organised a surprise party for me. It was brilliant. My birthday was on a Friday and we met after work for a drink in the city before she drove me home. She had her boys that week and they had gone to friends' houses for the night.

As we parked on my driveway, Alison told me that she needed to check on Riley as he had been a little under the weather. In reality the call was to one of the party guests to make sure everyone inside the house was ready. I completely fell for it. I walked into the house and saw a friend's head peeking out from a doorway. I still didn't twig what was going on. I just thought, *what's Darren doing here?* And then I got to the kitchen and there they all were. Local friends, work friends, the lot. I was gobsmacked, and amazed that Alison had known who to invite.

Sophie had spent the whole day home from school helping Alison to get ready—moving furniture and sorting out the food and drink. That morning Sophie and I had walked to the station together. We had said goodbye at the station entrance and moved to our respective ends of the platform—front of the train for adults, back of the train for schoolkids. Sophie had waited until I disappeared from view, and then simply walked home again.

It was a fantastic evening and I had a ball—I had never had

a proper party in my honour as an adult before. We even had a formal moment. Annabel welcomed the guests and then Sophie made a speech on behalf of herself and Annabel. I kept a copy of her words because they meant so much to me. This is what she said:

"Well firstly I would like to thank you all for coming tonight to celebrate our wonderful dad's birthday and for keeping it a secret. Also, Annabel and I would especially like to thank Alison for making this party possible because without all her help this wouldn't have been possible.

I think everyone realises what a wonderful person my dad is, especially over the last years of hardship. He has proven himself to be an even worthier father and someone who any parent can admire. Even after all the hours he works he still manages to do such a great job of looking after us and sometimes I think he forgets to give himself credit for all the hard work he puts in to making Annabel and my lives so wonderful.

I really can't find the right words to express my gratitude for you Dad because you really are just the best possible father ever and I feel like I can always come to you. Over the last years we have grown so much closer and you really are the person I admire the most."

It was a great moment for me and I was particularly pleased that my friends got to hear what my fifteen- and thirteen-year-old daughters thought about me—and to see how proud I was of them, and how proud they were of me.

31

Better together

Life with Alison was good. We would have a week of living together and then a week of living apart. There were good things and bad things about this. The good things list was quite long: it kept things fresh, we were always pleased to see each other after the week apart, we maintained our passion, we had our own space when we needed it and our relationship wasn't compromised by the issues of day to day life. The bad things list was a lot shorter. It really only had two things on it, but they were pretty fundamental—we missed each other during our week apart and Alison was becoming increasingly tired of moving between two houses.

As is natural for any couple, we started dreaming of the future. What would it be like to live together? Where would we live? How would the children cope? What impact would it have on our relationship? They were all good questions and we spent a lot of time talking about them.

One Sunday, on a cold winter's evening, Alison stood on the driveway of my house, her little pink overnight bag packed in her car, and I gave her my usual goodbye hug. She was back off home for another week.

This particular Sunday was different, Alison didn't let go. She wanted to keep hugging me and I felt her body start to shake. She was sobbing. Big, deep, emotional sobs. When she finally looked up at me, her face wet with tears, she told me that she hated saying goodbye and was finding our week-about routine harder and harder to deal with. She was torn. She loved going home to be with her children and she loved being with me. She didn't say it explicitly, but I knew what she wanted—to have me, Hayden and Riley in her life as much as she could and, what's more, she wanted us in her life at the same time. She'd had enough of her compartmentalised life. I just wanted to hold her.

I thought about it long and hard during the following week while we were apart. Maybe we should stop dreaming about the future and do something about it. I thought about my children. We had come so far on our travels together. I loved Alison, but my children were my first priority. I didn't want to put them through more difficulties and I didn't want to compromise my relationship with them. But, then again, how long should I keep on putting them first? They were getting older and more independent. In a few years time they would be adults and living their own lives. Was it time for me to think more about what I wanted? Was it time to ask my children to compromise a little?

Alison and I discussed the living together options. We both wanted to do it, believing it to be a natural extension of our relationship. There were only two things to get right, which sounded simple, but they would be critical to the success of our plans. One—where would we live? And two—how would we successfully create a blended family?

Question one was relatively straightforward. There were only two options. We could either stay in my house—with a bit of redesign/renovation it would be big enough to accommodate Alison and her boys. Or we could look for a new house. We knew finding a five or six bedroom house would be a challenge and so we very quickly realised that my house was the best way forward. We were sure we could design an extension that would provide everything we needed.

As for question two we had no idea—we didn't even know any other people running a blended family who we could ask for advice.

My management consulting training kicked in again. I suggested we develop a framework, or a set of principles, on which we could base our future life and use these to guide our decisions. Alison looked at me as if I was a complete tosser. I knew what she was thinking. How romantic was a framework or set of guiding principles? Wouldn't we get by on love, and the rest would then happily fall into place? Not in my book. I agree that without love there is nothing, but in this case I strongly believed that a good, solid framework would provide a platform for our new relationship. And guess what? I was right.

In any event, it didn't take long to put our principles together. I wrote them down on a piece of paper one night while we were out for a drink. I would love to say that I romantically scribbled them on a napkin which we took home and kept in our bedside table as a symbol of our new life. But I didn't. I took a piece of A4 lined paper with me and used that. Then I emailed our principles to Alison to confirm that what I had written down was what we had agreed. I love technology, and it *can* be romantic if used with care.

Our principles were:

1. The lifestyles of our children should not be compromised by our decision to live together.
2. We would each have 'alone time' with our children.
3. We would have 'alone time' with each other.
4. We would involve the children in major decisions.

5. We wouldn't force the children to become 'brothers and sisters' if they didn't want to.

And that was it.

I had another principle in my mind but I didn't mention it to Alison. I felt strongly that, if we were going to live together and build a blended family, we should get married. Call me old-fashioned, but living together would be a big commitment and getting married was, in my view, the proper and, dare I say it, 'traditional'—that word again—thing to do. And I wanted to set the right example for the children.

The next step was to use our principles to guide our decision on where to live. I was in heaven—the application of a set of principles to a real life issue is the ultimate high for a management consultant.

As with any piece of analysis it was best to start with the facts. My house was double-story and the girls lived upstairs, where they had their own bathroom and a living area. Downstairs there was a separate family bathroom, a study and a dining room—all rooms that were rarely used. The cheapest and quickest option to enable us all to live together would be to convert the study and dining room into bedrooms for the boys. They could then take over the family bathroom.

It was an attractive way forward but one which we discounted. The boys were also used to having their own living space upstairs at Alison's house, where they could hang out and get up to 'boy things' (I vaguely remembered these from my youth). Therefore this option would conflict with our principles—the boys would lose their personal space and their lifestyle would be compromised.

To keep true to our principles we needed to create effective zoning for the children. This meant the girls keeping their area upstairs and building a 'boy zone' onto the back of the house, so that the boys also had their own space. The existing family room would then become a shared area for us all to use as a blended family.

It was a more expensive option, but an investment we were happy to make. It was going to be a major change for our children and we wanted to make the transition as easy as possible. This meant everyone having a place to run to whenever they needed it, including ourselves.

Similarly, if we were to move to a new house, it would need to have comparable zoning. We knew this would be difficult to find. Most of the big five and six bedroom houses we looked at had most of the bedrooms upstairs, with one or two bathrooms and a living area. This would mean the children living on top of each other—and there were a whole host of reasons why that would be inappropriate.

So renovating and extending my house was easily the best option. Alison also felt that, because my girls had been through so much change already, it would be better for them to stay in their own home. But, in keeping with our principles, we would also get the children's thoughts in due course. In the meantime, we sketched out some rough plans as to what an extended house might look like. It was exciting, the first tangible step in designing our new future together.

Our other principles would be easier to put in place. We imagined that we would each take a long weekend away, once a year, with just our own children. We also agreed to have a regular dinner or movie night with them. We hoped this would help our children to understand that they were still part of a 'family within a family'. It would also make sure that we stayed in touch with them and how they were feeling—particularly in terms of what was working well and what could be changed.

As for the two of us, we committed to maintaining our 'date night' every other Tuesday and also going away for a weekend a couple of times a year. We resolved not to use the children as an excuse—getting time away together would be too important, especially with a larger family—and, as my girls were getting older, the option to leave them in charge of the house and the dogs was becoming more real.

So that was it. We had our foundations and we had our plans. We just needed to put them into place. Once again we were, deliberately, one step ahead of our children in our thinking.

The other issue in regard to the children was that they were going be a fundamental part of our future life together and yet they hardly knew each other. Hayden and Annabel had briefly 'gone out' in Year 5 at Primary School. It had all ended abruptly when Hayden asked Annabel for a kiss. She agreed, but only permitted a kiss on the cheek. Hayden took the cheek that was offered to him—and then made a move for the lips. And that was it. Relationship over before it had even started.

We recognised that it was important for the children to start spending some time together, to begin to get to know each other. So we instigated Sunday night dinners. The idea was simple. Every second Sunday night, at the end of her week at home with the boys, Alison brought Hayden and Riley round to my house for dinner. I cooked roast chicken, Alison made a fancy dessert, and we all ate together.

The dinners were successful from day one. The children had a ball and stayed at the table, rather than adopting their normal eat and run approach. It reminded me of the extended family dinners that I had enjoyed as a child. The conversation got louder and louder and the jokes and banter got ruder and ruder. On one particularly jolly Sunday night I told my joke about the scoutmaster and the dachshund, which unfortunately brought proceedings to rather an abrupt halt. But, apart from that, they went well. The children began to refer to our Sunday nights as 'family dinners', which was exactly the vibe Alison and I were trying to create. So much so that, when Alison and the boys left at the end of the evening, the house felt empty.

It was another small step in building a blended family.

32

Call off the search

The marriage thing was gnawing away at me. I'd had a wife for seventeen years, the majority of my adult life. Even though she had been living with another man for the last few years, had gone back to her maiden name and we were divorced, a part of me continued to think of her as my wife. I even frequently referred to her as my wife, rather than my ex-wife. Some things were hard to let go.

Did this mean I wasn't ready for another wife? Marriage was a massive step. Couldn't Alison and I do what so many other couples did and just live together? Was it essential to get married? If I got re-married would it be the first step on the slippery slope to becoming the next Henry VIII? What happened to his second wife? Oh yeah, beheaded.

But I loved Alison. I was ready to commit myself to her and I wanted to live with her. I also wanted to feel part of a broader family again. I realised it was unlikely that we would be able to create a traditional family life, but I hoped we could create something that was loving and supportive of its individual members. After all, regardless of blood-lines, isn't that a good definition of family? The commitment that Alison and I wanted to make to each other would have a huge impact on both the two of us and also our children. Marriage was the ultimate symbol of this commitment and so I was convinced it was the right way forward. And the more I thought about it, the more I realised that I wanted a formal occasion, involving our family and friends, to recognise our commitment. I just had to find the right time to ask Alison to marry me.

In my life to date I was sitting on a 100 percent success record in the 'will you marry me' stakes. I was one from one. My first marriage proposal may not have been the most romantic the world has ever known, but it was certainly effective—and, as with modern day sport, isn't it all about the result rather than the way you play the game? After all, the scoreboard doesn't lie, and mine was saying 1-0. My slightly off-hand line of "I think we should get married", while sitting on the beach at Mooloolaba was not particularly Shakespearian, but it had the desired result. Mind you, I paid the price over the following years as more and more of my ex-wife's friends regaled her with stories of their engagement moments—normally involving fancy, candlelit dinners, roses and distant views etc., etc. These did make my effort look a little bit shabby. I could probably do better second time around.

Or could I? Weren't those romantic engagements blatantly pre-planned and telegraphed? Didn't people see them coming a mile off? What about a complete surprise? Why not catch Alison off guard, at a time when she was least expecting it? That could be fun. I filed the thought away for future reference.

The other thing on my mind was Alison's own record in the 'will you marry me' stakes. She stood at an impressive 1-3. Her first husband had managed to extract the 'yes' vote on his first attempt but, subsequently, her 'special friend' had suffered from three failures, including one that involved a large diamond ring in a small box. It might take something special, or unexpected, to get through her solid and well organised defences. Still, Alison had mentioned that she would consider getting married again one day and I knew she loved me. So I felt confident I was in with a chance.

There were a couple of moments when I was on the verge of asking her. One afternoon, we were sitting outside in my back garden talking about, and trying to visualise, the house extension. It was a hot day and, as Alison was only guesting at the time, she didn't have her bathers with her. Her lack of appropriate attire meant that she was sitting in a T-shirt and her undies. In truth it was a bit of a daggy look—but at least it qualified as a 'she won't be expecting it' moment. We were talking about the future, what we could do with the house and the scale of the commitment. And I wanted her to know that I felt marriage should also be part of the bargain. So I got up and crouched down beside her chair. I didn't go for the full 'on your knees' approach, predominately because I thought it might be a tad corny, but also because I knew my knees couldn't take much more concrete action.

"What are you up to?" she asked me. "Are you going to try that kissing thing again?"

"No. I've been thinking about something," I replied, trying to stay calm.

Her eyes were scanning my face. I think she recognised a strange look in my eyes. She had seen this look once before when I rather unfortunately caught a snippet of my testicle skin in my zip, but this time the circumstances were completely different. She was beginning to anticipate what was coming.

"Don't," she said, a little harshly, and then more gently, "Not now."

I stood up. I understood the message. She wanted me to ask her, but not while she was sitting in a T-shirt wearing her everyday undies. It needed to be more special than that. Back to the drawing board for me.

Unfortunately, my clumsy, half-baked effort had given the game away. I wanted my proposal to be a surprise but Alison was now aware of what was on my mind and, no doubt, would be alert to situations when I might pop the question. A few date nights came and went. They were the obvious time, but for me they were too obvious. I also sensed that Alison was a bit tense when we went out for dinner, as though she was anticipating my proposal. And I wanted to ask her to spend the rest of her life with me when she least expected it.

A month or so later we went to Sydney for the weekend to attend the wedding of a work colleague of mine. It was a great opportunity to get away and have a bit of a party with some people I didn't see very often. I had worked a lot in Sydney before my separation and, after staying at the Sheraton on the Park for three months, I had managed to accumulate enough points for two free nights—very generous, these hotel schemes. The wedding was on Sunday evening, so we went up on Saturday lunchtime and planned to come back Monday morning.

I can't remember what arrangements I made for my children for the weekend—I just know it was during the school holidays. I can't even remember what we did on Saturday afternoon. But I do remember that we went for an early evening walk around the park and then got changed to go out for dinner. I hadn't booked anywhere, and we didn't intend to do anything extravagant anyway as we had a big night ahead of us on Sunday.

There is, however, a fantastic, small, cosy wine bar just along the road from the Sheraton. We dropped in there at about 7 o'clock and managed to get a little table down the back. I splashed out on two good glasses of red and, as this proved to be quite successful, two more. We were having a wonderful time, simply sitting close together in a romantic wine bar. And it came to me. This was a good time. It was spontaneous.

32 Call off the search

No preparation, no rehearsal. I just looked into her eyes and blurted it out.

"Will you marry me?"

I admit that I could have done better with my choice of words. A nice preamble reflecting on the times we had spent together and what Alison meant to me perhaps, or maybe painted a wonderful picture of our future together. But no, I just blurted out the textbook question. Classy.

Alison held my eyes for a moment but didn't say anything; she then put her arms around my neck and hugged me really tightly. I felt her body start to shake. I wasn't sure whether she was laughing or crying. It turned out to be a bit of both, but she was very happy. She told me how much she wanted to get married—but that she was in shock because she hadn't expected me to ask her at that moment. Bingo!

We were both very happy and very excited. That teenager feeling came back all over again. I thought we had been quite discrete with our emotions but the waiter came over to make sure we were all right. Being English, I told him everything was fine. Being Australian, Alison gushed that I had just asked her to marry me. The waiter was impressed and returned moments later with two glasses of champagne. Nice one. I took a card from the bar and wrote on it, "The rest of our lives started tonight". My scoreboard ticked over to 2-0. I started singing the soccer chant in my head.

The adrenaline rush had made us both hungry but unfortunately, because I hadn't booked anywhere for dinner, we had nowhere to go. After all, I hadn't planned an evening of engagement celebration. The only nearby restaurant I knew was a noisy, brightly lit Chinese place close to the hotel. I used to go there on my own quite a bit when I was working in Sydney as the food was pretty good. So that's where we headed.

It wasn't terribly romantic but we didn't care, we were totally wrapped up in our own dreams and plans.

Alison needed to tell one person before we ate. So she phoned her mum. I only heard one side of the conversation, which went something like this:

"Mum, I'm in Sydney and you'll never guess what's just happened…Mark asked me to marry him…No, Mark…the skinny Englishman…you *do* know him…that's right, the stalker…I said, 'yes', of course…okay…okay, I'll call you tomorrow."

"Is she all right about it?" I asked.

It hadn't sounded like a terribly convincing conversation from what I had heard. I had only met Alison's mother a couple of times and, apart from the initial, somewhat unfortunate, phone call to her, I didn't think things had gone that badly.

"Pretty much," Alison replied. "She's more used to me turning proposals down. She thinks it's a bit quick."

"Well it probably is a bit quick," I agreed. "But I totally believe it's the right thing to do."

"So do I," she beamed at me. And we held hands as we walked through the streets of Sydney.

I hadn't told anyone our news and didn't feel that I needed to. Alison thought I was holding back in case I wanted to change my mind later so, to show my commitment, I sent my brother a text. He called me back when we were in the middle of eating in the Chinese restaurant. He was delighted for me and said that my whole family would also be delighted. To them it was another step forward in me putting my life back together—albeit a rather large one.

"What did he say?" Alison asked me.

"He said 'congratulations'. And he told me not to give you too much to drink, in case the alcohol causes you to eat something that makes you ill and you end up in the back of an ambulance," I smiled. "Oh, and he thinks it's a bit quick."

We went back to the hotel. Use your imagination.

The next morning we were slow to surface. I love Sunday mornings when I'm away from home. They are completely relaxing and this one was no different. We had a late breakfast and then went for a cruise around the craft markets. I bought Alison a $10 gaudy ring to make things official. She bought me a medallion, which I love, although every other person I know thinks it's gay.

In the afternoon we travelled across Sydney to our friends' wedding. The ceremony was made more poignant by the knowledge that we would be having one of our own in the not too distant future. We resisted the temptation to tell everyone our news, it seemed rude to risk trumping the bride and groom on their big day, but it was too difficult to keep our excitement to ourselves and so we told a couple of my closest friends when we were at the reception. They were thrilled. They had supported me through the hardest period of my life and now they were with me at one of the happiest moments. It was beautiful symmetry.

33

Change the world

On our return to Melbourne, the next step in our journey was to tell the children. I genuinely had no idea how my girls were going to react. I knew another change in their lives might make them feel uncertain again, and maybe a little threatened. I was hoping they would be happy, but I would also completely understand if they weren't.

I told Annabel first. She was downstairs watching TV, Sophie was upstairs doing her homework.

"Annabel, I need to tell you something about me and Alison," I started, very carefully.

Annabel picked up on the serious tone immediately. She was ready for bad news.

"What is it?"

"It's something pretty big." I was skirting it a little.

"What is it? Are you breaking up?" She looked very worried.

"No," I smiled. "The opposite. I asked Alison to marry me."

"What did she say?"

"She said 'yes'."

Annabel broke out into a massive grin and started jumping up and down with excitement.

"That's so cool," she exclaimed. "I've never been to a wedding! Can I bring some friends?"

That was typical of Annabel. Always looking on the positive

side, always happy, always looking for a party. I loved her to bits. I had to wipe away a few tears.

"Have you told Sophie yet?" she asked me.

"Not yet. I'm about to."

"Can I tell her with you?" Her enthusiasm was infectious.

"I think I should tell her myself, but why don't you wait outside her door until I have done it?"

I was worried how Sophie would take the news. She liked Alison but she was still quite protective of me. It would be interesting. I took the same approach as I had with Annabel. Carefully, one step at a time. Sophie's reaction was very different. I noticed her eyes well-up.

"That's great Dad." A pause. "Where are we all going to live?"

And that was typical of Sophie. Calm, controlled, practical. I was so very proud of her. Another change for her to deal with, no doubt a daunting change, and yet she remained in control and aware. I knew that this girl would be able to cope with whatever life might throw at her.

I told her we hadn't yet decided where we would live; that it might be in an extended version of our home or it might be a new home. We would talk about it later.

Sensing the time was right, Annabel came bounding in still full of excitement.

"Isn't it great?" she asked Sophie.

"Yes," agreed Sophie, and she gave me a hug.

I was relieved. It had gone better than I expected. Annabel declared that we had to ring Alison to let her know how pleased she and Sophie were. What a girl!

Later that night, as I tucked them into bed, I asked them what they felt; now there had been some time for the news to sink in. For Annabel the initial excitement had worn off. She shed a few tears. She liked our little family of three and didn't want it to be broken up. I explained, as best I could, that she, Sophie and I would still be a family, and that she and Sophie would still be the most important people in my life. We weren't breaking up our family, I said, we were adding to it. I'm not sure whether I fully convinced her, but in the morning she was back to her normal self.

Sophie, as always, was more circumspect. She asked me lots of questions about where we would live, how often the boys would be with us, how the living arrangements would work, whether Alison would be in charge of the house and even whether we would eat the same food. Sophie liked the balance that we currently had with time on our own and our time with Alison. She seemed to be concerned about Alison's role as matriarch of our family and the potential for major changes to our way of life. Again, I explained that the three of us would still be a family unit. I also thought Alison's influence over my daughters would be a good thing—the girls needed a strong, female role model to supplement my parenting.

"Life's going to be different Sophie," I explained. "And at times it's going to be difficult. The most important thing is that we keep the bonds that you, Annabel and I have developed. I don't want that to change, regardless of whatever else changes."

"I'm happy for you, Dad," she replied. "It's just that every time I go to Mum's house there's someone else there who is not part of our family, and now it will be the same at our house."

I loved this girl so much. She had been so brave, she had been through such a lot and yet she had managed to keep it all together. She looked like a normal teenager from the outside. I hoped she was normal on the inside.

"I wish you'd told me," she said.

"Told you what?" I was confused.

"That you were going to ask Alison to marry you."

That took me by surprise. I didn't think I needed to ask my daughter's permission to get married. But it was indicative of the relationship I have with Sophie. We are close, and I think she felt that I had betrayed our closeness.

After a bit more thought, neither of the girls wanted to move house. They had a very strong preference to stay in their family home and for us to build a new zone for the boys. They liked their rooms and were comfortable in their surroundings. They wanted to minimise the change.

Meanwhile, over at Alison's house, things were going a little easier. Boys are much more straightforward. They weren't too concerned about the forthcoming wedding as long as they didn't have to wear 'gay suits' or do anything as part of the ceremony (they did wear suits but they weren't gay, and they did take part in the ceremony). Riley, the youngest, was very excited about moving into my house because of the pool and my Foxtel TV box. For him everything else was secondary. He went upstairs to sort through his stuff in anticipation of starting to pack. Alison had to remind him that they wouldn't be moving in until after we were married and the renovation was finished.

Later, he too, had more practical concerns. Both boys had noticed, on their visits to my house, a general lack of biscuits and other goodies. This was in stark contrast to the home life they were used to. Riley raised his concerns with me one evening.

"Mark, when we move into your house," he started, and hesitated.

"Riley, when you move in it won't be my house, it will be our house. It will be as much your house as the girls' house." I tried to help him out.

But I was completely off-beam with what he was worried about.

"Yeah that's good, but do you think we might be able to have a few biscuits?" he continued.

"Of course, your mum will have just as big a say about what we eat as I will." Bigger, as it turned out.

"Okay. And will I be able to have my friends over sometimes, if they don't get in the way or make too much noise?"

My heart went out to him. "Of course. It will be your home. And if it doesn't feel like your home then you should speak up. You and Hayden won't be visitors; you will be part of the family."

He seemed happier but I still didn't think he fully understood. It was a hard thing for an eleven-year-old to cope with.

And so it was done. We began to make plans for the renovation and for the wedding itself.

34

Never tear us apart

We had an absolutely brilliant wedding. Although we had both enjoyed our first weddings, our second one was different. It was *our* wedding and seemed to be more about *us* than our previous weddings were. Obviously, at its heart, it was still the two of us getting married of course. But this time, because we organised the whole day, we made sure that our wedding reflected our personalities and the 'feel' that we wanted. We found a magical venue, chose the food and drink, put together the guest list and table plan, decided on the type of service we wanted, wrote our own vows, chose our wedding celebrant and picked our own music. Our first weddings had represented a traditional (that word again!) approach to a marriage ceremony, this time it was much more personal—and a lot more relaxed.

We agreed from the outset that our wedding should also be about bringing two families together. And to reflect that we decided it should be a day for the children as well as a day for ourselves. We wanted to involve our children in the ceremony and, to help them celebrate; we wanted them to bring their friends.

The best news for me was that my mum, brother and sister were all able to come out from the UK. My brother was also my best man. I was pleased about this because he didn't make the cut at my first wedding and I had always felt a bit bad about it.

My brother and I sat in the front row of the chapel and, rather than being nervous, I was excited. We sat chatting and joking while the introductory music that Alison and I had put together played down. The background music came to a close and the opening bars of INXS's 'Never Tear Us Apart' rang out—our cue to take our positions at the front of the chapel.

First down the aisle were Annabel and Riley, arm in arm, followed by Sophie and Hayden, also arm in arm. The children joined me and Simon at the front of the chapel—a symbol to our family and friends that this wedding was about uniting two families, as well as two individuals. The children would stand with us throughout the service.

And then it was time for Alison to walk down the aisle, escorted by her brother. Every step she took brought her closer to me, and brought me closer to the end of my life as a single father. It had been an incredible and exhausting three years. Three years I had not expected. A lot of pain and a lot of sadness, but also moments of extreme happiness and some fantastic experiences with my children. I looked across at them and smiled. They smiled back. They were genuinely happy for me.

My mind rapidly ran through mental images of the times that the girls and I had shared. The moment when they had sat on the sofa while their mother told them about the break-up; the three of us coping with our sadness and confusion after our lives had been turned upsidedown; being strong for each other; the traumatic counselling session we had all attended; my awful early meals they had eaten so cheerfully; the drinking incidents; our strange and lonely Christmas; the moment the fog began to clear and we started to laugh again; and how welcoming they had been to Alison.

But most of all I thought of the bonds that the three of us had created. We had survived. More than survived, we had found out what it meant to be a true family. I loved them desperately.

And now I had Alison as well. I could never have imagined how positively my life would turn out. It was truly fantastic.

I knew that all of us were going to have to face, and deal with, a whole new set of issues as we built a blended family. But that was something for another day, today was all about celebrating.

I said my vows.

"Alison, I have known from the first time I met you that there is something special about you—and now I am extremely happy we have reached the point of committing our lives to each other. I am confident we will create a fantastic future for each other and our children. Therefore, before our families and friends I, Mark, take you, Alison, to be my wife. I promise to love you, to protect you, to respect you, to listen to you, to be your best friend and to be with you on every step of our journey. And I make this commitment in love."

Alison responded with her vows.

"Some people were just meant to find each other and I feel blessed that I have found you. I love you. I, Alison, take you, Mark, to be my husband. Today I join my life with yours and become complete. I promise to love you, cherish you, help and support you through whatever life may bring us. May the love we share today be everlasting and may our home be forever filled with love, happiness and contentment."

And a few moments later it was done. My life as a single father had come to an end.

My daughters

For me, the most important aspect of my life as a single father has been the relationship that I have built with my daughters. Through our pain and difficulties we all learnt about life together. I learnt how to be a single father and they learnt how to become teenagers and then young adults. And, as the dust and pain of separation eventually settled, we learnt to live as a family of three. We survived and found happiness in a new life together.

One of my girls found it much harder than the other. She is a lot like me. She is a deep thinker, broods on things, has a strong sense of right and wrong, and keeps her feelings bottled up inside her. At times she became a pressure cooker, her mind wrestling with her inner demons, as she struggled to work through her pain and anger. It was a terrible thing to live through with her. Sometimes she was unable, or unwilling, to open up to me or to explain what was troubling her and what she needed from me to make her feel better.

I have taken her to a number of counselling sessions. I have experienced a terrible sense of helplessness, sitting outside the counsellor's room, desperate to know what my daughter was talking about. In the early days, she would be visibly upset after the session ended and too exhausted to talk about it. It is one of the worst things a parent can go through. Parents want to help their children. Physical injuries can be repaired, but emotional difficulties are harder to understand and harder to resolve. My daughter took the break-up of our family very personally and has taken a long time to work through the consequences. However, she is an incredibly strong girl. I know she will eventually make sense of it all and find inner peace.

One of the huge positives from my divorce is that, as well as becoming close with me, the girls have also become very close with each other. I believe that the bonds they have formed as children will define their relationship as adults. My children support each other, confide in each other and love each other in a way that is unusual for teenagers. I know that I am close with my own family, but my daughters have a much stronger relationship than I did with my own siblings.

My daughters' bond has been forged in the sadness and uncertainty of a family break-up. They have had to come to terms with a completely different family life, witness the raw emotions of their parents and make difficult choices, often under pressure. It has given them great individual strength. I am enormously proud of them and hope that their experiences will provide a solid foundation for their adult lives.

Thanks girls, I love you more than I can put into words.

A daughter's perspective

I asked my eldest daughter if she would be prepared to express in words her memories of the moment when my wife told her, and her sister, that she was leaving us. These are my daughter's unedited words.

I didn't realise how quickly they could come out. The heavy rainclouds in her mind let loose their turbulent nature. They started the journey in bloodshot wells and swiftly swam down her cheeks to the base of her apple chin, finally falling to her lap, which would soon become very damp. As the words hit her ears, she fractured into many pieces that used to comprise my little sister. The sight of her fracturing broke my dad too. Then I thought to myself, why am I not crying? I sat there frozen, a mannequin in a window. They look real and you want to talk to them but they are plastic. I was not plastic though; I was real, but frozen in the words that I did not want to believe.

One in every three. That's the statistic for the number of marriages that end in divorce.

That moment in August changed my life, my sister's life, my family's life. Before my world broke apart I was with my best friend and nothing seemed complicated or unfair. Life was simple. We were kids and that was how it was supposed to be. Stress comes with age.

Mum called. She was picking us up. Normally we were allowed to go home at whatever time we liked. What was wrong?

A weird vibe filled the house when we walked through the

front door. It was as though the house knew something was coming and it was scared to breathe in case it gave it away.

Mum sat down on the 'good couch'. Then it began. The house had been right. Annabel and I looked as our mother, indestructible in our eyes, released months of built up pain. Cancer, I thought, she's dying. But still I did not move. I just watched as my mum crumbled, and as my sister started on the same track I wondered why my waterfall had not joined in the domino effect. I was a desert. Anger was taking over.

I became partially deaf as she started to explain. The words refused to be part of the sentences they were supposed to be forming. Maybe it was because I did not agree with the ideas that I couldn't comprehend them. But Annabel could. The words must have sunk deep into her mind the moment they touched her ears. Rushing, her tears ran away from her eyes as if scared to be kept there, yet mine were dry. Until Dad touched me.

A magician put him in the frame of the door, an upright corpse now out of place in a family home. He drifted over to me and the force of his hug was something I am yet to experience again. His unspoken words were projected through his touch, and that was all I needed. I understood.

The instant Mum sat on that couch and started to explain, my life changed. Its sad how little words can be so powerful, altering everything without physically doing so. Maybe if it had been the TV room couch I would not have been so overwhelmed by the news, the cookie crumbs unintentionally masking the life changing words coming from Mum's mouth.

But that is stupid. Nothing could have prepared me for that news. The news that my family, or 'family', was not going to be the same again, and that our 'family' holidays would consist of one parent. To me that's not family. Whether the couch was crumbed or almost unused would not have changed the fact that my mum was not in love with my dad.

For months, even years, there was always some part of me that could not understand how my own mother could intentionally change my life with the ease that she did. In my eyes she ruined us, the bond we had been creating and enhancing so easily taken away.

Perhaps maturity allows understanding, some things cannot be helped. Although I wonder what my life would be like if my parents were together still, it does not matter. At the time it seemed impossible for light to shine back through the window. Now, having two homes, I have many more windows for that light to shine in. My parents are both happy and have moved forward, my mannequin unfroze and my sister and I have never been closer.

Those months were dark but that doesn't mean every month has to be grey. There is always a silver lining; you just have to look for it. It helps with lots of windows.

Financial settlement: things to think about

Reaching financial settlement with my wife was a difficult and stressful process. There were a lot of things to consider and I learnt a lot. I have included some of my learnings here. I'm not a lawyer though, so treat this as my thoughts and not a legal opinion!

1. Asset Split
   As I mentioned in the book, there are a lot of factors that the Court can take into account in determining how the assets of a separated couple should be split. In my case, and I think in most cases, it comes down to the following:

   1. The responsibility of the ex-spouses for bringing up and maintaining the children.
   2. The relative earnings, and earning power, of the ex-spouses.
   3. Overall household earnings (in cases where one of the ex-spouses is now living with a new partner).

2. Chattels Spilt
   As part of our financial settlement my wife and I agreed a 50/50 split of our furniture and contents. It turned out that I got a bit fleeced on this.

   When my wife moved out she took with her some big bits of furniture, some kitchen stuff and a few mementoes—all things that she needed to start her new life. I was happy for her to do this. But here's the

catch. Our settlement agreement stated that she was entitled to half of the furniture and chattels in the family home. I didn't realised this meant half of the furniture and chattels that were in the house on the date of our settlement, so everything that she had already taken was deemed to be hers and she was now entitled to half of what was still left in our house.

This seemed to be outside of the spirit of our agreement. I should have read the ruling more carefully and taken it completely literally as the lawyers do. I was a bit miffed that my barrister didn't point out the impact of this clause, but then again he didn't know that my wife had already taken some furniture.

And that's another learning point: make sure your lawyer, and/or barrister if you are unlucky enough to need one of those as well, knows absolutely everything about your case so that they can spot potential pitfalls before it's too late.

3. Child Support

I have met a number of separated fathers who earn more than their ex-wives and have equal, shared care of their children. In these cases they have inevitably ended up with 40-45 percent of the financial assets on the basis that they are the higher earner. Following settlement, the ex-wife has then applied to the Child Support Agency (CSA) for financial assistance from her ex-husband towards her costs of raising the children. The CSA is a Government agency. The prime factor used by the CSA to determine the size of the child support payments between ex-spouses is their relative earnings. The agency does not take into account the way that the financial assets have been split or any informal agreements made between the ex-spouses about who will pay for what.

Therefore, there is a risk to the man of a double-whammy. It's likely that, because he is the higher wage earner, he has given his ex-wife a bigger share of their financial assets—and then he may get slugged for a large child support payment to his ex-wife because, guess what, he's the higher wage earner. It doesn't seem fair to me, although I can understand why it happens—the CSA needs a simple way of working out the required payments. And you can't ignore a CSA assessment because if you don't pay it they will take it from your wages!

My lawyer was aware of this. So we prepared a formal Child Support Agreement which specifically stated that the payments my wife and I made on behalf of the children, and for me my biggest one was school fees, would be offset against any future child support payments that the CSA might calculate. It all sounds a bit complicated, but basically it made sure that I was protected against any future claim by my ex-wife for additional money as a result of her applying to the CSA for child support.

4. Get It Done

It was a massive relief when the bulk of the financial decisions were over. I dragged my financial settlement out for a long time because it suited me, but this came with the price of significant emotional stress. My advice is that, unless there is a compelling reason not to, it's best to get the financial settlement over sooner rather than later. It brings a massive argument to a close, but don't worry, there will be plenty more! It means that you know where you stand financially, and that can be a relief.

You may have negotiated a good outcome or you may be unhappy with the outcome, but at least it's an outcome and you now know what position you are in. You know how much you can afford to spend on rent, or a new house, or paying your wife out to stay in your family home. You also know what your ongoing commitments to your children will be, you can make a new budget for the other costs in your life and you can begin to move forward. Your new life will start to come together from a financial perspective.

We need to do more for men

Having lived the experience, it is clear to me that men generally get a raw deal when it comes to separation and divorce—access to children can be difficult and the financial burden of supporting themself, their children and sometimes their ex-wife can be heavy. There is a general perception that men are unable to cope with raising a family on their own.

It's true that men are typically less well equipped than women to deal with life as a single parent, but should that be a surprise? A man's traditional role is to be the breadwinner rather than the homemaker. So when a man is suddenly required to perform both roles, without any training and with little support, it is obviously going to be a major challenge. But men are capable of doing it. We need to break the mould and recognise that men can, and indeed should, play a major and meaningful role in raising their families.

There is currently a lot of talk and activity aimed at improving work/life balance and creating flexibility for women to help them to manage the competing demands of their career and raising a family. It's time to acknowledge that a large number of men are also performing both roles. We need to be more proactive in supporting those men who choose to be, or find themselves, in this position and help them to make a success of both aspects of their lives.

The Music

(The soundtrack to the book!)*

1.	Dazed and Confused	Led Zeppelin
2.	Leaving Me Now	Level 42
3.	And Then There Were Three	Genesis
4.	Welcome to the Jungle	Guns N' Roses
5.	Sunday Bloody Sunday	U2
6.	Stiff Upper Lip	AC/DC
7.	Eye of the Tiger	Survivor
8.	Band of Gold	Freda Payne
9.	Absolute Beginners	David Bowie
10.	Let's Talk About Sex	Salt-N-Pepa
11.	Message in a Bottle	The Police
12.	Beautiful Girls	Van Halen
13.	Girls on Film	Duran Duran
14.	I Want You to Want Me	Cheap Trick
15.	Something About You	Level 42
16.	Blame it on the Moon	Katie Melua
17.	Happy Xmas (War is Over)	John Lennon
18.	Can't Fight This Feeling	REO Speedwagon
19.	Slide it In	Whitesnake
20.	Rock On	David Essex
21.	Relight My Fire.	Dan Hartman
22.	Love to Keep You Warm	Whitesnake
23.	London Calling	The Clash
24.	I Hear You Knocking	Dave Edmunds

25. Money	Pink Floyd
26. D-I-V-O-R-C-E	Tammy Wynette
27. Perfect Strangers	Deep Purple
28. Burn	Deep Purple
29. Who's That Girl?	Eurythmics
30. Love Shack	The B-52's
31. Better Together	Jack Johnson
32. Call Off the Search	Katie Melua
33. Change the World	Eric Clapton
34. Never Tear Us Apart	INXS

*Not available in any good record shops.

The final word

I hope that this book has been both helpful and entertaining for all single fathers. There is no magic wand that you can wave to make yourself a successful single father, neither is there a simple recipe for success. The most important thing is to stay strong and work on it day by day.

Be confident, because although it seems daunting, it is possible. You will find strength you didn't know you had, and go on to achieve things you never thought possible. Separation is a terrible thing for you, your children and your (ex)-wife, but, although it won't feel like it at the time, it is also a tremendous opportunity and a chance to grow. And, after all, you have no choice—you have to accept your new life. Embrace it, don't run from it.

Your new job is a simple one. It is to be the best dad that you can be and to give your children the best life that you possibly can.

And the greatest thing of all is that your children will love you for it.

www.ingramcontent.com/pod-product-compliance
Lightning Source LLC
Chambersburg PA
CBHW032035150426
43194CB00006B/292